ON DISTANT SHORE

Part 4

January 21, 2016 - June 2, 2016
In descending order

Val G. Abelgas

Published and printed

by TATAY JOBO ELIZES.
Self-Publisher
in 2017, under the
permission and authorization
of VAL G. ABELGAS,
author and owner of the copyright to this book. The copyright owner can withdraw this permission at his discretion without any objection from Talay Jobo Elizes at any time. Printing of this book is using the present day method of Print-On-Demand (POD) system, where prints will never run out of copies to be available for posterity. The copyright owner is free to republish with other publishers anytime.

ISBN - 13: 978 - 1976418365
ISBN - 10: 1976418364

Disclaimer: Views are expressed by the author alone. Tatay Jobo Elizes does not knowingly publish false information and may not be held liable for the views of the author and right to free expression.

Contact: job_elizes@yahoo.com
Website: http://tinyurl.com/mj76ccq

Special Note

Articles are arranged in reversed chronology descending from newer dates to older dates

About the author

VAL G. ABELGAS
Publisher-Editor, Philippine Post
Editor, www.thepinoyweekly.com
Columnist, On Distant Shore
valabelgas@aol.com

Val G. Abelgas, Publisher and Editor-in-Chief of the Los Angeles-based Philippine Post, has been a professional journalist for almost 45 years, 20 of them in Manila and 25 years in Los Angeles.

Val started as a sportswriter in the now defunct Philippine Daily Express in 1972 while still in his junior year in journalism at the University of the Philippines' Institute of Mass Communications. He rose to become city editor of then the country's biggest daily newspaper at a very young age of 24. He was the last managing editor of the Daily Express, which was closed down by the Cory Aquino administration in 1987. The next day, he moved to the Manila Standard as its first managing editor.

After stints as editorial consultant of the Philippine Star Group and later managing editor of the Philippine Times Journal, he and his family immigrated in 1991 to the United States, where he later obtained his green card as an alien of extraordinary ability in the field of journalism. In his first year in the US, he was editor of the Los Angeles Monitor and the next year became the first editor-in-chief of Balita. He moved to the Philippine Times in 1993, during which time he won the Newspaper of the Year and Columnist of the Year awards of the Philippine Press Club of America for two straight years in 1993 and 1994. In November 1993, he organized the first-ever nationwide convention of Filipino-American editors in Los Angeles with President Fidel V. Ramos as guest speaker. In 1995, he left the Philippine Times to join his wife Marisse in editing the Philippine Post and later became editor of Ang Peryodiko, the Pinoy Weekly and the Philippine Tribune. He published and edited two magazines with his wife, the Philippine Post Magazine and the Hiyas Magazine.

Before becoming a professional journalist, Abelgas was editor-in-chief of The Nucleus, official organ of the Manila Science High School, assistant news editor of the Philippine Collegian, official newspaper of the University of the Philippines, and editor-in-chief of the Campus Journal, laboratory newspaper of the UP-IMC.

Abelgas wrote a column, "As We See It," for the Philippines Daily Express in the 1980s. In 1992, he started writing his weekly "On Distant Shore" column, which is being published in 9 Filipino publications in the US and Canada.

Val has won numerous journalism awards both as a professional and campus journalist and served as director of the National Press Club of the Philippines five times and president of the Philippine Press Club of America. In 2016, he was named Journalist of the Year by the Filipino-American Press Club of California. He has travelled to more than 30 countries in official assignments as a journalist.

ooooo

Contents

ooooo

1
Federalism: Caution wouldn't hurt
June 2, 2016

IT IS ALMOST certain President-elect Rodrigo Duterte will push hard to amend the Constitution to replace the country's current unitary form of government to one that is federal. After all, he launched his drive to the presidency on the pretext of an information drive on the federal system of government in nationwide sorties long before the presidential campaign started.

It is false to assume, however, that the more than 15 million people who voted for him chose him because of his pro-federal system stand. He rose to national prominence based on his tough drive against criminality and corruption and he won by a landslide because of that. Majority of those who voted for him probably don't even understand what federalism is all about and what it means to the country.

Even with his overwhelming popularity, Duterte will have a tough time selling the concept to the people and to the members of Congress, who will decide whether to constitute itself as constituent assembly (con-ass) or to legislate the creation of a constitutional convention (con-con) to amend the charter.

Duterte may find it easier to sway the House of Representatives with his coalition suddenly gaining close to 300 turncoats, but he is certain to face a stronger challenge in the Senate, the more thinking chamber.

Senate President Franklin Drilon and Senate president pro-tempore Ralph Recto said the proposal needs comprehensive study on its impact on national policies and that any effort to amend the Constitution – a necessary step for a shift to federalism – involves a tortuous process.

"What are the details of federalism, how will it affect taxes? How will it affect the division of natural resources?" Recto asked, adding that lawmakers and policy makers should ponder these questions if federalism would be discussed.

But it's not just the issue of taxation or division of natural resources that need to be discussed if a shift is to be made. Federalism is a complete stranger to Filipinos and jumping into it would not be as easy as 1-2-3 or as elementary as A-B-C.

Proponents of federalism love to point to the United States and Malaysia as examples of highly successful federal countries. But they also forget to mention that these countries did not start as one nation. Writer Michael Henry Ll. Yusinco stressed that federal states such as the US, Malaysia, Australia and Germany all began as "a loose collection of disparate political entities that gradually, and with painful upheavals, transformed themselves into a unified nation-state through the process of federalization."

He added: "It would essentially be the reverse in our case. Consequently, we face a much harder, more complicated, and possibly harsher version of federalization. It is thus disconcerting that purported advocates of federalism seem oblivious to the gravity of this sociopolitical reform. They quickly harp on the promise of enhanced local autonomy without even considering the readiness of the local leadership to assume the big responsibility of local governments under federalism, as if the fitness of the current crop for this form of government were already a given."

We have had a brief look at having an autonomous state in the failed experiment called the Autonomous Region of Muslim Mindanao (ARRM) that only spawned a stronger, abusive political dynasty in the Ampatuan clan, an even chaotic governance, and an economy that insured the ARRM became the poorest region in the country.

As clearly demonstrated by the Maguindanao example, federalism will further strengthen political dynasties. There is no denying that established political clans have been in control of local politics for generations. With greater powers under a federal set-up, what will stop them from further solidifying their hold on Philippine politics? A regional, instead of national elections for senators, would put more of these political dynasties at the national helm by being elected to the Senate.

Yusinco also contends that the shift to federal form of government would not succeed with political dynasties still entrenched in our political system. He pointed to a groundbreaking study by the Asian Institute of Management Policy Center in 2012 titled "An Empirical Analysis of Political Dynasties in the 15th

Philippine Congress," which showed that lower standards of living, lower human development, and higher levels of deprivation and inequality persist in the communities governed by political dynasties.

Former national treasurer Leonor Magtolis-Briones, who has been picked by Duterte to head the Department of Education, said in her article entitled "Financing Federalism," said: "Students of public finance have been pointing out that the creation of an additional layer of government—namely the state—will inevitably lead to higher levels of expenditures. This is because the machinery of the states has to be maintained, along with that of the federal government and the local government units. Pressure for higher levels of expenditures will inevitably lead to pressure for increased levels of taxes."

For example, each of the proposed 11 states would have its own supreme court, parliament, Cabinet departments, state police, etc. that would necessarily entail huge budgets.

A federal form of government will create additional layers of bureaucracy that will lead to even more red tape, corruption and confusion. Businessmen and investors will be the most adversely affected as they will have to contend with conflicting and confusing laws from various states/regions. Can you imagine 11 states with their own agencies on commerce and industry, housing, health, transportation, education, etc. and the federal government having its own, too, all with their own sets of rules?

Instead of unifying the country, federalism could further divide the country. Ilocanos have long considered themselves a people distinct from the Tagalogs, and so do the Visayans, the Muslims, the Bicolanos and other regional tribes or groups. Just when these groups are beginning to blend as one, we now say they are groups distinct from one another.

If one state becomes more progressive and more powerful than the others, what will stop it from moving to secede from the union and become a truly independent entity?

With not much help from the central government, regions with very little natural resources and existing infrastructures are almost certain to lag behind, negating the primary reason proponents are pushing for federalism. Proponents say federalism would enable each state to grow on its own by using its own resources, taxation and leadership.

Under the present form of government, provinces are given proportional revenue allocations under the Internal Revenue Allotments (IRA). Metro Manila gets the biggest share not because the national government is based in Metro Manila, but because the region has the biggest contribution to the country's gross domestic product (GDP), accounting for a more than 36-percent share.

These are just some of the problems that could confront a sudden shift to a federal form of government. I also agree with Yusinco that the political consciousness of Filipinos must first be elevated before a sudden shift to a federal form of government.

Duterte and the other proponents of federalism may be right that the shift could be the solution to the country's many problems. But they could also be wrong.

It would be to the best interest of the country that the proposal be discussed more lengthily and more cautiously before we jump into it. It's an issue that could make or break the country. A little more caution and introspection wouldn't hurt.

Ooooo

2

Reject re-imposition of death penalty

May 30, 2016

THE DEBATE over the reimposition of the death penalty in the Philippines was revived last week after President-elect Rodrigo Duterte said he would ask Congress to allow public executions by hanging as part of a ruthless law-and-order crackdown that would also include ordering military snipers to kill suspected criminals.

The tough-talking Davao city mayor said capital punishment by hanging should be imposed for heinous crimes, and criminals convicted of killing, robbery and rape should receive "double the hanging."

"After the first hanging, there will be another ceremony for the second time until the head is completely severed from the body," he said. This is an overkill, of course, often used by Duterte to excite his audience during the presidential campaign.

While his derring-do was hailed by several supporters, including Dante Jimenez of the Volunteers against Crime and Corruption (VACC), the proposal was met with strong opposition from various groups.

It is easy to be carried away by the euphoria of promised change, but with the election over and the real work at hand, let us be more careful in assessing radical proposals presented by the incoming leadership. But let's go back to the plan to reimpose the death penalty.

The Philippines is one of 139 countries all over the world that have abolished the death penalty from their statutes. It is the only country in Asia that does not impose the death penalty.

The country has at one time or another suspended or resumed capital punishment.

Capital punishment was banned by the 1987 Constitution in the Philippines except for certain heinous crimes. In 1993, during the term of President Fidel V. Ramos, the death penalty was revived although the first execution was carried out by lethal injection during the term of President Joseph Estrada. In 2000, Estrada called for a moratorium on the request of his spiritual advisor, Bishop Teodoro Bacani.

On April 15, 2006, Congress passed Republic Act 9346 that re-abolished the death penalty and in June that year, President Gloria Macapagal Arroyo commuted the death sentences of 1,230 death row inmates to life imprisonment of a minimum of 30 years.

In 2012 following the gruesome killing of UST honor graduate Cyrish Magalang, who was stabbed 49 times in Cavite, the VACC pushed for the revival of capital punishment as a deterrent to crime.

Proponents of the death penalty all over the world cite its role as a major deterrent to crime as the primary reason capital punishments should be imposed. However, such claims have no basis in fact. In the Philippines, for example, according to Sen. Joker Arroyo, a longtime human rights lawyer and activist, the revival of the death penalty from 1993 to 2004 did not bring the number of violent crimes down.

In the US, Texas has had the most number of executions for years, but is still ranked 13th in the country in violent crimes and 17th in murders per 100,000 citizens.

The American Civil Liberties Union said there is no credible evidence that the death penalty deters crime more effectively than long terms of imprisonment.

"States that have death penalty laws do not have lower crime rates or murder rates than states without such laws. And states that have abolished capital punishment show no significant changes in either crime or murder rates," it said.

There is no evidence that serial killers and rapists would consider their death by lethal injection or in the gas chamber prior to committing crimes. Law enforcement experts say criminals usually operate with the belief they will not be caught.

Proponents also claim that "deserved punishment protects society morally by restoring this just order, making the wrongdoer pay a price equivalent to the harm he has done." Abolitionists, however, counter: "To kill the person who has killed someone close to you is simply to continue the cycle of violence which ultimately destroys the avenger as well as the offender."

The biggest argument against the death penalty, however, especially in the Philippines where the judicial system is far from ideal, is the real possibility that a wrongly convicted person could be put to death for a crime he did not commit but was unable to defend himself in court because of various factors, including inadequate legal representation by court-appointed defense attorneys, serious flaw in police investigative work, racial prejudice, political pressure to solve a case, and misrepresentation of evidence.

It is the poor who can't afford to hire the best lawyers and who often have to rely on public defenders that end up in death rows, unable to defend themselves and nobody willing to listen to their protestation of innocence.

Even in the US, which boasts of one of the best judicial systems in the world, it has been established that two out of three death penalty convictions have been overturned on appeal because of police and prosecutorial misconduct.

Proponents of the abolition measure in California cited the case of Cameron Willingham who in 2004 was executed in Texas for a fire that killed his children. Impartial investigators established later, however, that there was no arson involved and that Willingham was wrongly convicted.

US Senator Russ Feingold of Wisconsin, in introducing the National Death Penalty Moratorium Act of 2000 said: "It is a central pillar of our criminal justice system that it is better that many guilty people go free than that one innocent should suffer… Let us reflect to ensure that we are being just. Let us pause to be certain we do not kill a single innocent person. This is really not too much to ask for a civilized society."

In the Philippines, which has one of the worst law enforcement and judicial systems in the world that even President Aquino once expressed his doubts on the ability of courts to render fair judgments, one can just imagine how many in its Death Row really deserve the capital punishment.

Abolitionists suggest that instead of death penalty, those convicted of certain violent crimes should instead be sentenced to life imprisonment without the possibility of parole and made to work while in prison, with a big portion of their pay given to victims or victims' kin as payment of court-ordered restitution.

In the US, opponents stress that the death penalty brings heavy financial burden on states and counties because of the lengthy and expensive jury trials and sentencing trials. Aside from these costly trials, those sent to Death Row are allowed endless appeals that also cost tens of thousands of dollars. In the meantime, they are given free board and lodging in county and state prisons and often die anyway before they are executed.

The death penalty, especially public hanging, is a senseless, barbaric form of state-aided revenge that has long been abolished by civilized society. That many American states have continued to embrace it is ironic for a country known as the leader of the modern world.

The Philippines, on the other hand, gained international recognition when it abolished the death penalty in 1987 and 2006, the only country in Asia to do so. Why join the ranks of the uncivilized again?

Ooooo

3

House of turncoats
May 27, 2016

WHY AM I not surprised that despite having just three members in the House of Representatives, the PDP-Laban is almost certain to have control of the chamber?

With the election of Davao City Mayor Rodrigo Duterte, the official candidate of the PDP-Laban, to the presidency, the small party headed by Sen. Koko Pimentel has suddenly become a magnet to the old and new members of the coming Congress. Politicians are suddenly shifting their allegiance to Duterte and his party. After all, that's what political chameleons do. They change colors as often as political expediency dictates.

Just a few days after it was certain Duterte would be the next president, people and parties of all shades and colors started trooping to Davao City to hopefully partake of the spoils of the recent political war.

First to shift allegiance to Duterte was the Nationalist Peoples Coalition (NPC), the country's second biggest political party and the party with the biggest number of House members.

NPC president Isabela Rep. Giorgidi Aggabao said the party has committed to support Duterte's legislative agenda, which includes the reinstatement of the death penalty and the amendment of the 1987 Constitution to change the country's system of government to federal, and the speakership bid of incoming Davao del Norte Rep. Pantaleon "Bebot" Alvarez, who is Duterte's choice for Speaker of the House.

The NPC, which was a member of Aquino's "Daang Matuwid" coalition in the House, had supported the candidacy of independent candidate Sen. Grace Poe and just as soon as Poe lost, became a Duterte ally.

Next in line for a share of the political booty was the Nacionalista Party, headed by former Senate President Manny Villar. The NP was also a member of the Liberal Party-led coalition in the House. With the entire Villar clan by his side, Duterte announced that he would appoint Las Pinas Rep. Mark Villar as secretary of the Department of Public Works and Highways.

Villar's appointment was met with strong criticism from friends and foes alike, including longtime friend and ally Pastor Apollo Quiboloy, but everyone knows there are no permanent friends in politics, only permanent interests. And so Villar's appointment stays in exchange for control of Congress.

Next in the Davao queue were the Lakas-Christian Muslim Democrats, the original party of the present-day political chameleons; the National Unity Party, a breakaway group of the Lakas-CMD; and the 45-member bloc of party-list representatives.

And guess who came next in the rush to join Duterte's Coalition of Change? A group of 45 Liberal Party representatives, who are abandoning Aquino even before he steps down from office on June 30 and leaving a handful of party loyalists, led by incumbent Speaker Sonny Belmonte, to tend the store for LP, which suddenly becomes the minority party.

Guess whose name we saw in that bunch of LP turncoats? A former governor who was the chief apologist of then President Gloria Macapagal Arroyo, was, as I suspected, in the group. When he was elected congressman at the same time as Aquino became president, he turned Liberal and became one of Aquino's chief apologists.

With the movement of the balimbings, Alvarez, Duterte's anointed and a one-time congressman way back from 1998 to 2001, is suddenly assured of becoming the next Speaker of the House of Turncoats, also known as the House of Representatives.

Why the exodus from the Liberal Party? Aside from the fact that nobody wants to be a part of the losing party, at stake in the division of the spoils are six seats for Deputy Speakers, and chairmanship of 57 committees and 20 special committees.

And, of course, a share of the congressional and presidential pork barrels, which although already declared illegal and unconstitutional by the Supreme Court, eventually find a way to get into the annual national budget.

The frequent political movements by these political turncoats are normal phenomenon in Philippine politics abetted by the onset of the multi-party system under the 1987 Constitution. With parties lacking clear ideological delineations and their members lacking principles, members change party loyalties in the name of political expediency, or what these politicians call "political resiliency."

I'll repeat here what I said in a previous column ("Poltical chameleons," June 15, 2015):

"The instability of these political coalitions reflects, and contributes to, the instability of the country's political system. Because these parties were formed primarily for the vested interests of its founders and leaders, they are devoid of ideology and platform of government. The parties change stands on issues, and shift loyalties as often as political exigency demands. They change color as they wish like the chameleons.

"Because they are based on the self-serving agenda of the leaders, parties tend to change platforms depending on what can win them votes at the time, or what can be advantageous to their own objectives. The needs of the people that they are supposed to serve are often overlooked. And because the members join the parties not because of the party's ideals and principles, there is no loyalty on their part and they become political butterflies, moving from one party to another in the same manner that parties move from one coalition to another.

"If the parties and the party members cannot be loyal to their own ideals or their own parties, how can they be expected to be loyal to the people?"

Ooooo

4
"Daang matuwid" comes to a dead end
May 20, 2016

WITH Davao City Mayor Rodrigo Duterte winning by a landslide over President Aquino's anointed candidate Mar Roxas, it's obvious "daang matuwid" has come to a dead end. After all, Aquino has repeatedly said the 2016 presidential election is a referendum on how the people rate his administration's performance and whether or not they want "daang matuwid" to continue for the next six years.

His so-called "bosses" themselves put a roadblock to "daang matuwid" by ignoring Roxas and turning instead to a tough-talking political outsider for radical change that they had hoped would be achieved by Aquino's "kung walang corrupt, walang mahirap" mantra.

Aquino had stomped the campaign trail in the last few weeks to push for victory for Roxas and his "daang matuwid," even claiming in the last week of the campaign that he is the best president the country has ever had in terms of solid performance.

Obviously, less than one-fourth of the voters believed him because only this much percentage voted for his anointed candidate.

While Aquino boasted of the success of his administration in the last week of the campaign, on the same breath Sen. Miriam Defensor Santiago was calling "daang matuwid" the "ultimate frustration" of the Filipino people. Sen. Grace Poe, who refused to say anything negative against Aquino for most of the campaign, said people are disillusioned with the Aquino administration's "daang matuwid" governance because of its failure to provide decent public services.

Even Roxas had to acknowledge the Aquino administration's many mistakes towards the end of the campaign when he told the voters during a rally: "I know deciding whom to vote for will not be easy for you. Maybe you have chosen other candidates already. But we also know that the government has its shortcomings and that your complaints are valid."

Roxas promised to correct the mistakes of Aquino's "daang matuwid" in an apparent, albeit belated, effort to dissociate himself from his friend Aquino, who has proved to be a baggage instead of an effective endorser for his presidential bid.

The former senator from Capiz must have realized by now that he should have campaigned independently of Aquino and presented his own program of government instead of promising to continue the President's failed "daang matuwid" program.

Aquino's "daang matuwid" failed on the very first day of his term when he ignored tradition and took his oath before then Associate Justice now Ombudsman Conchita Carpio Morales, the lone dissenter in a Supreme Court vote that ruled that the two-month ban on presidential appointments did not cover the judiciary. If he followed tradition, he should taken his oath before Chief Justice Renato Corona.

It was clearly a vengeful act against the SC decision that deprived him of the right to appoint the Chief Justice. As it turned out, it was only the first of many clashes Aquino had with the high tribunal, a co-equal branch of government, that reached its crescendo with Corona's impeachment.

Aquino used every available forum to embarrass Corona, including one where he lambasted the Supreme Court's decisions right in front of Corona, and revived the issue of the midnight appointment although the tribunal had already ruled on it.

Why the hatred for Corona and the Supreme Court? Aquino apparently could not forgive the justices for stopping his first two executive orders that Law Dean Fr. Ranhillo Aquino described as "negative in tenor and vengeful in intent" – the one recalling the appointment of thousands of employees he labeled as midnight appointees and the other creating a Truth Commission that would have enabled his administration to conduct a witch hunt of the officials of the previous administration.

But there was an even more important decision that eventually led to Aquino's displeasure over the Supreme Court and to Corona's impeachment. In a unanimous resolution, the SC had ordered the distribution of the 4,915.75-hectare Hacienda Luisita, which is owned by the Aquino-Cojuangco clan, to the original 6,296 farmer-beneficiaries. Three weeks after that landmark decision, Corona's impeachment began.

By then, his vengeful acts against Corona and his alleged use of pork barrel funds to make the congressmen and senators follow his orders of impeaching the Chief Justice had drowned out his initial gains in the shallow "wang wang" policy.

Until now, Aquino cites the impeachment of Corona, the imprisonment of former President Gloria Macapagal Arroyo, and Senators Juan Pone Enrile, Jinggoy Estrada and Bong Revilla on plunder charges as the highlight of his "successful" campaign against corruption. And yet, he cannot explain why he was fast in defending his closest aides in the Cabinet – Transportation Secretary Emilio Abaya, Agriculture Secretary Proceso Alcala and Budget Secretary Florencio Abad – when these three bulwarks of the Liberal Party were embroiled in corruption scandals.

It became obvious that the "daang matuwid" was only applicable to his opponents while his friends and allies were free to thread the dark, crooked path of corruption without fear of imprisonment. It was a clear case of "selective justice" and Aquino couldn't care less about such criticisms.

If indeed the "daang matuwid" were a straight path for everybody that would eliminate corruption and remove the stumbling block to poverty, why then was the government plagued with so many corruption scandals during his term, from the lowly "tanim-bala" at the airports, to rice smuggling, to the gigantic pork barrel anomalies involving the Priority Development Assistance Fund (PDAF) and the Disbursement Acceleration Program) that were ultimately ruled unconstitutional and illegal by the Supreme Court?

Other events that would forever sully Aquino's legacy were the Luneta hostage crisis in the first month of his term that exposed to the world his new government's ineptitude; the tragedies wrought by super typhoon Yolanda and the siege of Zamboanga city by Muslim rebels that showed his administration's incompetence and lack of compassion; the Mamasapano massacre that resulted in the death of 44 elite policemen and showed that this government was not only inept and indifferent but is also capable of covering up the truth; and the brutal dispersal of farmers asking for relief from hunger in Kidapawan that ended with three farmers dead and 53 injured, which showed the government's lack of apathy for the poor's plight.

Aquino had raised the bar high and yet failed to deliver. He had raised the people's hope too high and let them slam back to the ground with his unfulfilled promises.

And he is surprised that the voters opted for radical change instead of pursuing his failed "daang matuwid"?

Ooooo

5
Now, let the healing begin
May 13, 2016

THE people have spoken.

Based on initial results from the Commission on Elections, the tough-talking Davao City Mayor Rodrigo Duterte is on his way to landslide victory in the May 9 presidential elections and will thus become the country's president starting noon of June 30.

As of this writing, Duterte was leading administration candidate Mar Roxas by more than six million votes, so far the highest margin of victory in a presidential election held under the 1987 Constitution, higher than President Benigno S. Aquino III's lead of 5.7 million over former President Joseph Estrada in 2010. Percentage-wise, however, Aquino's 42.08 percent share remains the highest in the post-martial law era.

With almost 74 percent of the votes counted and his margin further increasing with new votes coming in, there is no way Roxas or independent candidate Grace Poe can catch up or even close in on Duterte.

Realizing the inevitable and in a class act, Poe conceded defeat to Duterte and promised to help in the healing process for a nation that was for months leading to the election has been severely divided by one of the, if not the most contentious presidential election in recent Philippine history.

"Binabati ko si Mayor Rodrigo Duterte at ipinapangako ko ang aking pakikiisa sa paghilom ng ating bayan at pakikiisa ng ating mga kababayan tungo sa patuloy na pag-unlad ng ating bansa," said Poe, who lived in the United States long enough to witness losing candidates conceding within minutes of the tabulation.

Poe's running mate, Sen. Chiz Escudero, followed suit and conceded defeat in the vice presidential contest, where Liberal Party candidate Camarines Sur Rep. Leni Robredo was nursing a slim 100,000-vote lead over independent Sen. Bongbong Marcos. This contest was headed to a photo finish.

Escudero, who led in surveys in the early part of the campaign, was languishing in fourth behind Robredo, Marcos and Sen. Alan Peter Cayetano.

Sen. Antonio Trillanes, who was in distant fifth and who tormented Duterte in the last week of the campaign with allegations of hidden wealth against the Davao mayor, conceded Duterte has won the election "clearly and convincingly" and pledged that he would not stand in the way of reforms to be initiated by Duterte.

"I respect the will of the Filipino people. They have spoken clearly and resoundingly that they want Mayor Duterte to be our next president," Trillanes said. "I assure the Mayor and our countrymen that I will not be a hindrance to the reform initiatives he intends to push in our government."

These are class acts shown by Poe, Escudero and Trillanes and I hope that the other losing candidates would follow suit and make their covenant with the people to respect their voice and contribute to the long healing process that should follod this naturally divisive democratic process.

"Vox populi, vox Dei." The voice of the people is the voice of God. The "bosses" have spoken resoundingly and unequivocally.

President Aquino should lead officialdom in respecting the voice of the people, whom the outgoing president has repeatedly called his "bosses." The President, who staked his legacy by declaring that this election is a referendum on his "daang matuwid" governance, is the biggest loser in this contest because Duterte's victory is a clear and resounding rebuke of his claim that he is the best president the country has ever had in terms of solid achievements.

Aquino stomped the campaign trail to pitch for Roxas and Robredo and his "daang matuwid" governance. When it became obvious that Duterte was headed to victory, Aquino called on Roxas and Poe to agree to unite to stop the Davao mayor. But neither Roxas nor Poe, understandably, was willing to withdraw after going through a grueling campaign.

Aquino should make up for his loss of face with a magnanimous act by leading his party mates in congratulating Duterte for the victory and pledging to help heal the nation.

I hope that Aquino and his Liberal party mates would be gracious in defeat and not initiate any plot to defy the people's voice, such as seeking to disqualify Duterte on technicality. Remember that the Comelec decided to overlook the fact that the Davao mayor substituted for PDP-Laban party mate Martin Dino, who for some reason wrote in his Certificate of Candidacy (COC) that he was running for Pasay mayor instead of for president.

There is a chance that Roxas, on the prodding of Aquino, may file a protest before the Presidential Electoral Tribunal (PET), a judicial-legislative body that has exclusive jurisdiction over presidential electoral protests. The tribunal could declare Roxas the winner by the PET based on this technicality.

While this may have legal basis, I hope that Roxas and Aquino would respect the voice of the people or his "bosses."

Another possible scenario that I hope the Liberals would not resort to unless totally justifiable is what Marcos calls the party's Plan B where Robredo wins the vice presidency through poll tabulation manipulation and then the LP-controlled Congress would move to impeach Duterte after a few months and Robredo becomes president.

Please, Mister President. Vox populi, vox Dei. The bosses have spoken. No more dark conspiracies.

With the victory of Duterte and possibly of Robredo, who may both be considered political outsiders because of their lack of national exposure and nationwide base, the people have shown their despise for traditional politics or for the way the government has been run by the usual elective officials for decades.

The election has also shown that the voters are now more independent-minded and more conscientious about their votes as shown by the surprise ascent to the top of the Senate race by TESDA chief Joel Villanueva, the victories of independents Dick Gordon, Migs Zubiri and Risa Hontiveros, and the poor performance of showbiz/TV celebrities like Alma Moreno, Mark Lapid, Edu Manzano and Rey Langit.

After months of acrimonious campaign that has divided families and friends as can be gleaned from the unending debates in the social media, it is paramount that the winners focus on healing the nation. No more exchange of threats and expletives. The winners should show they are magnanimous in victory and the losers that they can be gracious in defeat. This should include the candidates' supporters.

The people have spoken. Let us all respect that.

Ooooo

6
A change not to be relished
May 5, 2016

IT SHOULD be a time of hope for millions of Filipinos as they prepare to go to the polls on Monday, May 9, to elect the new set of leaders who will govern the country in the next six years.

The last six years had not turned out as we had hoped when we elected the son of a recently deceased revered democratic icon. After six years of hypocrisy and ineptitude, the hope has turned to despair, and the promise of deliverance from corruption and poverty under President Benigno S. Aquino III's "daang matuwid" has remained just that, a promise.

The coming presidential election should offer us hope, as all electoral processes should, but looking at the line-up of contenders for the presidency, it seems the people are left to choosing the one with the least baggage, or the one who will bring us to the least doom, or the one who just might be able to bring the radical change that many think the nation needs, at whatever cost.

The utter frustration of the people on the ills that have kept the country from attaining real, sustainable and inclusive growth has made them too defeatist to think that all politicians are corrupt anyway so why worry about corruption allegations against some of the candidates, or too desperate to risk giving up freedom and democracy in exchange for radical change, or too naïve to allow another candidate to pursue the broken promises of his benefactor or to put a totally inexperienced aspirant holding the reins of government.

Surely, there must be better options for national leadership out there. But alas, we have to contend with the five that were thrust to us for this election.

So, who should we elect on May 9?

I cast my vote on the first week of the voting period for overseas absentee voters, but I must admit that it was a reluctant choice for president. The candidate is, to my humble estimation, the best in the lightweight list of presidential aspirants.

Nonetheless, one of them will become the next president of the Republic of the Philippines. We had hoped for a miracle when we elected Aquino six years ago. Apparently, it did not happen. We need another miracle for one of these five candidates to deliver the promises that they have been dishing out in their campaign sorties – eradicating crime, corruption and poverty.

It seems one of them, Davao City Mayor Rodrigo Duterte, does not need any miracle. He says he just needs six months to weed the country of criminals and corrupt elements, a feat none has accomplished in the 70 years since the Americans allowed us to govern ourselves. He said he would fill Manila Bay with bodies of criminals and the corrupt. If the congressmen and senators try to impeach him or block his program of change, he wouldn't hesitate to abolish Congress or declare a revolutionary government.

He boasts of having many girlfriends, jokes about the rape and murder of an Australian missionary, and dishes out expletives at every turn. And yet, if surveys are to be believed, more than 30 percent of the people will elect him to become the next president of the Philippines.

If that is not a resounding rebuff of Aquino and the political establishment or a clear sign of frustration and desperation, I don't know what is.

I can understand the anger, the frustration and the desperation of the people. We all feel the same way. But decisions solely based on anger, frustration and desperation are often not the best decisions that we can make. Such decisions can often lead to even more disappointment, frustration and anger.

But who else is there to trust our country's future to? Sen. Grace Poe does not have the necessary experience to lead a country confronted with, among others, corruption, crime, poverty, terrorism, rebellion in the South, and an alarming conflict with China over islands in the South China Sea. Worse, her and her husband's loyalty to the country has been questioned because of Niel Llamanzares' past employment with an outfit that has contracts with US intelligence agencies.

Vice President Jejomar Binay's credibility and integrity have been seriously challenged by the numerous accusations of graft while he was mayor of Makati. While he may have the experience and the capability to lead the country, claims of corruption will hound him throughout his term, possibly rendering him ineffective.

Former Interior Secretary Mar Roxas may be the best candidate in terms of preparation and academic credentials, along with Sen. Miriam Defensor Santiago, but he has nothing new to offer, except the continuation of Aquino's failed "daang matuwid."

He also carries a baggage of failure and lack of sensitivity in the departments that he handled as a member of the Aquino Cabinet – the Department of Transportation and Communications and the Department of Interior and Local Government. The image of the government's lack of immediate and adequate response to the Yolanda disaster and the Zamboanga siege, and the LRT-MRT mess is enough to dissuade the people from believing he can deliver on his promise.

Santiago is brilliant and totally prepared to lead the country after his successful stints as judge and senator, but it would be difficult for the people to entrust the presidency to her because of her serious illness.

There is not much promise of redemption from these candidates, and yet we have to make a choice. It is paramount that we consider foremost the character of the candidate, as suggested by Philippine Star columnist Dick Pascual. Some say strength as a leader should be given emphasis. Others say experience is a must. Others say mental aptitude is important.

Although there have been many changes in survey frontrunners, Duterte obviously not only has a commanding lead of from 9 to 12 percentage points over Poe, but also has the momentum that could carry him to victory on May 9.

Under these circumstances and sans any kind of poll fraud, Duterte could be our next president. If Duterte lives up to his current image, Filipinos could be getting the change they may not necessarily relish, either by martial law or another People Power uprising. Déjà vu!

Ooooo

7
Embracing Duterte, warts and all
April 28, 2016

THE RISE in the presidential surveys of Davao City Mayor Rodrigo Duterte is short of phenomenal and comes just two weeks before the May 9 elections. While the ratings of all his rivals are either sliding down or unmoving, the Davao demagogue has continued to surge and leave his rivals eating dust.

In the Pulse Asia survey, conducted from April 12-17 at about the same time the furor about his joke about the rape and murder of an Australian missionary in a Davao City jail in 1989 was starting to take shape, the tough-talking Duterte garnered 34 percent of the votes of some 4,000 respondents nationwide, and further widened his lead to 12 points over erstwhile frontrunner Sen. Grace Poe, who got 22 percent.

While Duterte gained two points from his previous rating of 32 percent in the April 5-12 poll, Poe, who has problems of her own regarding the citizenship and loyalty of her husband Neil Llamanzares, dropped by three points from 25 percent.

Vice President Jejomar Binay of the United Nationalist Alliance, who had regained the lead just a few weeks ago, slipped one point and was three points behind Poe at third with 19 percent. Administration and Liberal Party candidate Mar Roxas, who has never gained any kind of momentum since the campaign began in February, remained flat and fourth with 18 percent.

Independent candidate Sen. Miriam Defensor Santiago, who did well in the two presidential debates despite her poor health, was last with 2 percent and was not expected to move any higher with only two weeks to go.

Apparently, personal campaigning by President Aquino and his celebrity sister Kris has not helped the cause of Roxas. The funny thing is despite his languishing in the cellar for several months, Roxas insists he remains confident of victory and that the most important survey result is on May 9.

Either Roxas knows something we don't know, or he's just too arrogant to accept that he is headed to a resounding defeat, which can only mean an even more debilitating defeat for his friend and benefactor Aquino, who has repeatedly said that the May 9 election is a referendum on whether or not the people want his "daang matuwid" reform agenda to continue for another six years.

The biggest wonder here is that despite the obvious immorality and vulgarity of the tough-talking Duterte as shown by the remark that he made – taped on video and witnessed by millions of Filipinos courtesy of the internet – about the rape and murder of an Australian missionary, he continues to gain support from even the supposed decent sector of society.

The missionary, who was ministering in a prison in Davao City, was taken hostage, raped and killed during a riot by inmates in 1989.

"They raped all of the women … There was this Australian lay minister … when they took them out … I saw her face and I thought, 'Son of a bitch. What a pity … they raped her, they all lined up. I was mad she was raped but she was so beautiful. I thought, the mayor should have been first," Duterte was shown in the video telling a crowd of laughing supporters at a campaign rally.

The remark drew widespread indignation from his fellow candidates, women's groups and from other celebrities in social media, including American Ambassador Philipp Goldberg and Australian Ambassador Amanda Gorley.

But Duterte obviously rode out the furor as he maintained a nine-point lead over Poe in the Social Weather Station survey, which was conducted on April 18-20, a day after the rape remark furor went viral on social media.

Support for Duterte, in fact, climbed to 33 percent in the SWS April 18-20 poll from 27 percent in the March 30-April 2 survey. Poe remained in second place with 24 percent voter preference with nine points separating the two. Roxas overtook Binay in third spot with 19 percent, from 18 percent in the previous survey. Binay was down to 14 percent, from 20 percent. Santiago had two percent voter preference.

How will they stop Duterte if not even a comment that "dapat nauna ang mayor" in taking liberty with the beautiful Australian missionary could stop his followers from choosing him over more decent and more qualified candidates?

At least in the vice presidential survey, Aquino's party is getting a better deal with LP bet Rep. Leni Robredo, who for much of the time was also lagging behind independent candidate Sen. Ferdinand Marcos Jr. and erstwhile front runner Sen. Chiz Escudero, surging past her two more prominent rivals.

Robredo had 26 percent – up seven points – against Marcos' 25 percent – down one point – in the SWS April 18-20 survey, but they are in a statistical tie for the top spot.

Escudero fell to third place with 18 percent from 21 percent, followed closely by Sen. Alan Peter Cayetano with 16 percent from 13 percent.

Senators Antonio Trillanes IV and Gregorio Honasan II remained at the bottom, garnering five percent and two percent, respectively.

However, in the SWS survey, conducted on April 12-17, Marcos remains the frontrunner. Marcos took the solo lead with 29 percent. Robredo was in second place with 23 percent, followed by Escudero, with 20 percent. Cayetano,

Duterte's running mate, had 16 percent. Honasan and Trillanes remained at the fifth and sixth slots with four percent and three percent, respectively.

Again, the constant call of President Aquino to condemn martial law by voting against Marcos seems to have fallen on deaf ears as the young Marcos has a six-point lead over Robredo in the SWs survey and statistically tied with the Bicol congresswoman in the Pulse Asia poll.

As I said in my March 7 column ("Why Duterte and Marcos are contenders"):

"It is a source of wonder why 30 years after Filipinos staged a peaceful revolt to oust a dictator, many of them now seem eager or willing to embrace a presidential candidate who threatens to impose a strongman rule and a vice presidential aspirant who is the namesake son of the supposedly hated leader they deposed in what is now known as People Power Revolution.

"I am surprised to this day that many people, even from the so-called civil society, are supporting either Duterte or Binay for president and Marcos for vice president. I know many doctors, lawyers, journalists and other professionals who swear to high heavens that Duterte is the kind of leader the country needs. Another group swears Marcos could make this country "great again." And others believe that despite all the graft cases against him, Binay is the one who could lift the masses from poverty.

"One explanation is that some or many of the people who gathered on EDSA from Feb. 22 to 25, 1986 have been utterly disappointed that another set of oligarchs and dirty politicians have taken over the reins of the country and have not brought the hopes and aspirations of EDSA to reality. Thirty years later, the government is back to "business as usual" and the poor and the middle class remain ignored and forgotten."

I can't find of another reason why for all his faults, except that the people are so desperate for a new leader that they are willing to embrace Duterte, warts and all.

Ooooo

8
Let us heed the call to vote
April 21, 2016

LAST Thursday, I performed my duty as a dual Filipino citizen by voting as an overseas voter in the Philippine Consulate General in Los Angeles. I had planned to wait for my absentee ballot in the mail, but I decided to see first hand how the new automated election system worked.

It was so easy and so efficient that it took just a few minutes to pick the candidates for president, vice president and 12 senators plus one party-list, have the ballot scanned by a machine, verify the votes from a printed voter receipt, and put back the receipt in a designated box. It seemed easier than the voting in US elections, where I have been casting my vote since the 2008 presidential elections as an American citizen.

If you live within driving distance to the Philippine embassy or a consulate, I suggest you don't vote by mail but in person so that you would understand the process better and personally feel the joy of being able to have a voice in charting the future of our beloved homeland.

I have to congratulate the staff of the Philippine Consulate General in Los Angeles, headed by Consul General Leo Herrera-Lim, consul Mary Joy Ramirez, the Comelec-designated election officer, and Cultural Officer Wilma Bautista for their efforts to inform the community about the new automated process, to encourage registered Filipino voters to go out and vote, and to make the voting process as comfortable and enjoyable as possible.

Voting for the 1,376,067 Filipinos who registered for overseas absentee voting for the 2016 national elections started last April 9 and will go on until the local equivalent of 7 p.m. Philippine time on May 9. If you don't want to fall in line, don't wait for the last day and go to your consulate the earliest possible.

The Commission on Elections is targeting an 80-percent turnout for the absentee voters, a lofty goal that must be tried nevertheless. If by a stroke of miracle the goal is met, it would mean more than 1.1 million overseas voters would actually cast their votes, which is certainly more than enough to make a difference in deciding who would be the next batch of national leaders who will lead our country through the next six years.

With political pundits predicting the closest presidential and vice presidential races ever, the 1.3 million overseas votes – not counting the number of votes overseas Filipinos can influence – could spell the difference between victory and defeat for these national candidates. Even from afar, overseas Filipinos can be a major factor in the course that the country will pursue in the next six   years.

In the 1992 presidential elections, for example, Fidel Ramos won by only 874,348 votes over Miriam Defensor Santiago in a seven-way fight among major candidates. In 2004, Gloria Macapagal Arroyo won by 1.12 million votes over Fernando Poe Jr. in a fraud-marred election highlighted by the "Hello Garci" scandal. Arroyo's running mate for vice president, Noli de Castro, bested Loren Legarda by only 881,744 votes. In the 2010 elections, although Benigno Aquino III beat Joseph Estrada by 5.7 million votes, Estrada's running mate Jejomar Binay won over Manuel Roxas III by only 727,084 votes. But if the two previous elections were to be the gauge, the 80-percent turnout goal would seem not only lofty, but would be closer to the realm of the impossible dream. In 2010, voter turnout was 26 percent or 153,323 voters, while in 2013 it was only 16 percent or 118,823 voters.

It is hoped, however, that with the unprecedented interest in the current campaign, which is the most contentious thus far, more overseas Filipinos would troop to the polls this time.

The first four days of overseas voting did not offer hope of even getting close to the 80-percent turnout. The Department of Foreign Affairs reported that as of 7:30 p.m., April 12 (Philippine time), only 27,620 have voted so far.

As usual, Hong Kong registered the highest number of voters with 9,167 as of 2:30 p.m., Monday, April 11, followed by the Middle East and Africa with 7,159, Europe with 1,927 and the Americas with 107. The 107 from the Americas, which include the US, Canada and the rest of the continent, is certainly disappointing but it is hoped that the number would geometrically increase as the voting deadline nears and as the mailed ballots start coming in.

During a briefing at the consulate in Los Angeles , Consul General Herrera-Lim said the absentee ballots would be mailed to out-of-state voters in the very first week of April and to those in Southern California in the second or third week of the month.

Thirty out of the 85 foreign service posts will implement the automated election system, which covers about 1.12 million voters. These posts are those in Abu Dhabi and Dubai in the UAE; Beirut, Lebanon; Doha, Qatar; Jeddah, Al Khobar, and Riyadh in Saudi Arabia; Kuwait; Manama, Bahrain; Tel Aviv, Israel; Hong Kong; Kuala Lumpur, Malaysia; Osaka and Tokyo in Japan; Seoul, South Korea; Singapore; Agana, Guam; Chicago, Honolulu, Los Angeles, New York, San Francisco, and Washington D.C. in the USA; Ottawa, Toronto, and Vancouver in Canada; London, United Kingdom; Madrid, Spain; and Milan and Rome in Italy. The automated election system makes it a lot easier for voters to cast their ballot, and this should encourage overseas voters to participate in this year's crucial elections.

Leaders of overseas Filipinos all over the world, especially here in the United States, fought a long and hard battle to gain voting rights for those who cannot go back to the Philippines to vote. There have been four elections since then, and we still have to show that it was worth the struggle and the expense on the part of the government to give us back the right to help determine the destiny of our beloved country.

As Filipinos who have seen how democracy works in their adopted countries, especially in the US and other developed nations, and have a more objective view of what is happening and what is good for the homeland, it is hoped we could provide the more intelligent votes for this election. We can protest the corruption and impotency of the national government back home but if we remain indifferent and stay away from actual participation in the country's elections, all these would not matter.

Ooooo

9

Why leave citizenship issue hanging?

April 13, 2016

THE RECENT ruling by the Supreme Court upholding its earlier decision reversing the Commission on Elections' disqualification of Sen.

Grace Poe has removed all obstacles for her to run in the May 9 elections. But apparently, it has not removed the possibility that Poe may be disqualified later on by the Presidential Electoral Tribunal (PET) if she's elected.

While she was allowed to run, there was no explicit and final ruling from the high tribunal on the issue of her citizenship as questions remain on whether the 7-5-3 vote (7 justices saying Poe is a natural born citizen, 5 saying she is not, and 3 refusing to rule on the issue) could be considered final.

The seven justices who voted to declare Poe a natural-born Filipino were Chief Justice Maria Lourdes Sereno, and Associate Justices Presbitero Veleasco, Lucas Bersamin, Jose Mendoza, Marvic Leonen, Jose Perez and Francis Jardeleza.

The five Justices against it were Senior Associate Justice Antonio Carpio, Associate Justices Teresita Leonardo De Castro, Arturo Brion, Bienvenido Reyes and Estela Perlas Bernabe.

Associate Justice Mariano Del Castillo declined from giving an opinion while Associate Justices Alfredo Benjamin Caguioa and Diosdado Peralta disagreed with the majority when it proceeded to vote on the citizenship issue.

Senior Associate Justice Antonio Carpio is insisting that the tribunal failed to reach the eight votes needed to grant a petition filed before it. Under the Supreme Court's internal rules, if all 15 justices deliberated and voted on a case, a majority of 8 votes is required in granting a petition. Carpio said no justice inhibited from the case but Sereno interpreted the positions of Del Castillo, Caguioa and Peralta as non-participation and non-voting.

"Since there is no dispute that there are only seven justices who declared that petitioner is a natural-born Filipino citizen, there is clearly no majority vote on the issue of petitioner's citizenship. Seven votes is less than a majority. Accordingly, there is no majority sustaining petitioner's status as a natural-born Filipino citizen. In short, the issue of petitioner's citizenship remains hanging and unsettled," Carpio said.

Justices De Castro, Brion and Reyes believe that the ruling would jeopardize the conduct of the election and even stressed that a victory by Poe would not erase the questions on Poe's eligibility.
"The delay in the ruling on citizenship will only invite instability in the conduct of the coming elections," De Castro pointed out.

Brion hinted of a possible Presidential Electoral Tribunal case due to the failure of the high court to settle the legal issues on Poe's qualifications. He said no legal bar exists for a qualified petitioner to question Poe's qualifications after the elections should she win.

Reyes agreed that here was no majority ruling that Grace Poe is natural-born citizen and that foundlings found here are natural-born Filipinos.

With Sereno stressing that the court would no longer entertain any appeal or motion on the matter, it now appears that the issue on Poe's citizenship would be left hanging until the elections .

I can't understand why the Supreme Court could not break the impasse on the citizenship ruling. If the justices could take a 9-6 vote on the residency issue and on allowing Poe to proceed with her candidacy by overturning the Comelec cancellation of her COC, there is room for Cagouia and Peralta, who both voted with Sereno, et al to allow Poe to run and in dismissing the motion for reconsideration, to finally agree to vote to get the needed majority decision.

Caguioa and Peralta didn't want the court to proceed in voting on the citizenship issue until the Presidential Electoral Tribunal had made its determination. But that would mean a Supreme Court majority ruling wouldn't be coming until after the election, and only if Poe wins and somebody brings the matter to the PET.

The situation has given credence to rumors quietly circulating among opposition circles that the administration would allow Poe to run, which could create a situation where the LP could claim that Poe snatched votes from the other opposition candidates, and enable poll fraud operators to slip Liberal Party standard bearer Mar Roxas into second place behind Poe.

Roxas would then file a protest before the PET questioning Poe's qualification based on the same reason of not being a natural-born citizen. The Presidential Electoral Tribunal, which is composed of the Chief Justice and the associate justices, would then proceed to disqualify Poe, and Roxas would be declared the duly elected president. Neat, isn't it?

I can't understand why Caguioa and Peralta insist that it is the PET and not the SC that should make the determination whether to disqualify Poe or not based on the citizenship requirement when the PET is the same Supreme Court that reconstitutes itself as the Presidential Election Tribunal to decide on protests involving the presidential and vice presidential elections.

Is it being done intentionally and maliciously? Is the Supreme Court being used to suit the machinations of political powers as claimed by some sectors?

Why wait until after the elections to decide on such a critical constitutional question as to whether foundlings are natural-born citizens or not? The question raised on Poe's citizenship after all constitutes a constitutional issue that only the Supreme Court can decide with finality.

I agree with several sectors that the high tribunal should do it before the May 9 elections to avoid any potential constitutional crisis and possible political instability later on.

Ooooo

10
Shameful indifference
April 6, 2016

WHY IS IT that every time farmers take to the streets to air their legitimate grievances, they are met with violence in the hands of the government that professes to exist to serve them? Why is that when the poor protests, they are met with bullets and batons, instead of compassion and understanding?

We ask these in the wake of the violent dispersal last Friday of 6,000 hungry farmers who gathered on a highway in Kidapawan City in North Cotabato to demand 15,000 sacks of rice for as many families who have been suffering from hunger because of the drought. They were hoping to stir the government to action. Instead, they met a violent reaction.

Instead of listening to their problems, hundreds of policemen, on orders of the mayor and the tacit approval of the governor and perhaps of higher officials in Manila, bombarded them with water cannons and shot them with M-16 rifles. In the aftermath of the brutal dispersal, three farmers lay dead, 53 were injured and 60 more protesters were missing.

For three days, the farmers stood on the highway fronting the National Food Authority warehouse, where thousands of sacks were probably lying idle, hoping that the government would take compassion and give them the one sack of rice per family that they were asking to tide them over while their elected officials busied themselves campaigning for reelection on the same old promise of helping and uplifting the poor.

The farmers were simply demanding that the provincial government fulfill its promise to assist them during the drought. They were simply asking that the officials they helped elect would take pity on them and their families while they await government action on the extended drought that has prevented them from growing rice and other crops.

But compassion obviously is lacking in most of our wealthy officials. Neither is tolerance in their vocabulary. It was almost certain the protest would be met with brutality in the same deadly manner the government reacted to the legitimate protests by peasants and farmers who marched on Mendiola street in Manila on Jan. 22, 1987 to demand that President Cory Aquino fulfill her campaign promise to implement agrarian reform and distribute farmlands to farmers.

Twelve marchers were killed, 39 other protesters suffered from gunshot wounds, and 12 others sustained minor injuries. They were first blasted with water cannon and then met with a hail of bullets.

Or as brutal as the way policemen and soldiers dispersed the rally of thousands of farmers in Hacienda Luisita – yes, the sugar lands owned by the Aquino-Cojuangco families in Tarlac – on Nov. 16, 2004. The farmers were demanding that the farmlands be distributed to them as required by the Agrarian Reform Law. When the smoke settled, seven farm workers lay dead on the land they had tilled for decades, 121 were injured (32 had gunshot wounds), including 11 children and four elderly men. In the succeeding weeks, eight supporters of the strike were killed: Bishop Alberto Ramento, former supreme bishop of the Iglesia Filipina Independiente; Fr. William Tadena, also of the IFI; Tarlac City councilor Abel Ladera; Ric Ramos, president of the Central Azucarera de

Tarlac Labor Union; and four worker-community leaders. These murders have not been satisfactorily resolved to this day. "It is vile enough that this administration has failed to support the farmers and lumad of Kidapawan during the prolonged drought in Mindanao. But it is downright inhuman for them to shoot at the same people begging for help," Sen. Miriam Defensor Santiago said of the latest act of oligarch brutality.

"In the first place, there would not have been a protest if only these people felt compassion from their leaders. This government cannot claim to be pro-poor when it answers pleas for help with bursts of gunshot," the senator added. Vice President Jejomar Binay, through his spokesman, also assailed the violent dispersal of the hungry farmers. "They asked for rice, but they got bullets," said spokesman Rico Quicho. "Hunger is a reality that must be addressed not by violence but by compassion and concrete programs to improve the lives of the poor." Senator Francis Escudero said every citizen has a right to free assembly, and that the concerns of the farmers were legitimate. "The least the government could do is listen to their concerns and do something about it," he said. The Promotion of Church People's Response, on the other hand, expressed "utter contempt for hardhearted leaders who answered the people's cry for food with death-dealing bullets and stone-hard blows."

"When the hunger of the poor brings violent responses from those in leadership, these leaders are not fit to govern," said Marie Sol

Villalon, PCPR co-chairperson. "Our government is plagued with shameful indifference." Amid the maelstrom, President Aquino kept silent.
The Kilusang Magbubukid ng Pilipinas (KMP) said Aquino's silence on the violent dispersal of the farmers was reflective of his "habitual practice" as a "landlord president" of dismissing farmers' demands.
"Aquino's continuing silence and the lines mouthed by his numerous mouthpieces betray the President's official position both on the issue of drought and the Kidapawan massacre. Aquino's deafening silence shows that he is used to violent dispersals and massacres as a habitual practice of the landlord president in dismissing farmers' just, legitimate, and moral demands," KMP chair Rafael Mariano said.
What can you expect from an administration that didn't show any compassion for the 44 elite policemen killed in the Mamasapano massacre, or for the thousands of victims of super typhoon Yolanda in Tacloban, or for the millions of SSS pensioners who were seeking a P2,000 increase in their monthly pensions to give them relief from the scourge of inflation?
As one militant said: "Our government is plagued with shameful indifference."

Ooooo

11
Disempowering political dynasties

March 30, 2016

THREE news articles that appeared in the past week highlighted the sorry state of our political system – the prevalence of political dynasties all over the country.

One news item reported that 542 candidates in the local elections are assured of victory because they are running unopposed. Most, if not all, of these unchallenged candidates are members of entrenched political dynasties. The most prominent of these unopposed candidates are former President and two-term Rep. Gloria Macapagal Arroyo of the Macapagal-Arroyo clan of Pampanga; and Gov. Imee Marcos of the Marcos clan of Ilocos Norte.

The Macapagal-Arroyos of Pampanga and Negros Occidental have produced two presidents (Gloria and Diosdado Sr.), one vice president (Gloria), one senator (Gloria), three congressmen (Ignacio, Diosdado and Mikey Arroyo) and vice governor in Cielo Macapagal-Salgado.

The Marcoses of Ilocos Norte have produced a president – Ferdinand, who ruled for 20 years – two governors (Imee and Ferdinand Jr.), senator (Ferdinand Jr.), two congresswomen (Imelda and Imee) and their other relatives (the Barbas and Keons) have also dominated Ilocos politics for decades.

Another prominent political family is that of former President and now Manila Mayor Joseph Estrada of San Juan and Manila, who, however, is being challenged by former Mayor Alfredo Lim.

The Estrada-Ejercitos have produced one president (Joseph), one vice president (Joseph), four senators (Joseph, Dr. Loi Ejercito, Jinggoy and JV Ejercito), five San Juan mayors (Joseph, Jinggoy, JV and Guia Gomez) and two Pagsanjan mayors (ER Ejercito and wife Girlie), Laguna governor (ER Ejercito), Quezon board member (Gary Estrada), and one councilor (Jana Ejercito).

The second news item that showed how entrenched political dynasties are is the story on the proclamation rally of Rep. Abigail "Abby" Binay, who is running for mayor of Makati. The entire Binay clan – Vice President Jejomar Binay, who is running for president; Sen. Nancy Binay, dismissed Mayor Junjun Binay, the matriarch former Mayor Elenita Binay, and Abby's husband Luis Campos, who is running to replace his wife as congressman. The proclamation rally became a family affair just as Makati has become the Binay family's fiefdom.

The third news item showed the powerful Garcia clan of Cebu holding a press conference where the Garcias announced that they were junking Binay, whom they had endorsed just one week earlier, because the Vice President attended the political rallies of the Garcias' political rivals in the province.

Political dynasties have been described as "machineries of power that seek to perpetuate their own bloodlines and expand their reach."

One reason political dynasties have continued their domination in their respective political territories is that because of their positions of power and influence, national officials and those seeking national positions, and businessmen operating or wanting to operate in their areas of control have to kowtow to these powerful political clans.

And because these elite families have both political and economic control over their provinces or cities, people outside of their circle of influence who are otherwise more qualified, more honest and more dedicated to render public service are unable to win elective positions.

"The problem with elite politics is there is no program or platform, it's all power," said Ramon Casiple, executive director of the advocacy group Institute for Political and Electoral Reforms.

"A lot of these political dynasties feel they own the seats that they occupy and it's theirs to bequeath, to whoever family member they see fit," anti-corruption group Transparency and Accountability Network executive director Vincent Lazatin said. "It is very disturbing."

It is indeed disturbing. Consider these facts from Wikipedia:

• From 1995 to 2007, an average of 31.3% of all congressmen and 23.1% of governors were replaced by relatives. Of the 83 congressmen elected in 1995 to their third term, 36 of them were eventually replaced by a relative in the succeeding elections.

• In a study done in 2012 by economists, it was estimated that 40% of all provinces in the

Philippines have a provincial governor and congressman that are related in some way.

• A 2014 study done by Prof. Querubin of the Department of Politics in New York University indicated that approximately 70% of all jurisdiction-based legislators in the current Congress are involved in a political dynasty, with 40% of them having ties to legislators who belonged to as far as 3 Congresses prior. It also said that 77% of legislators between the ages of 26-40 are also dynastic, which indicates that the second and third generations of political dynasties in the Philippines have begun their political careers as well.

For decades, political dynasties have ruled Philippine politics. With the ascension of the late Corazon Aquino to the presidency in 1986 after the EDSA People Power revolt, it was hoped that democracy would be given a total rebirth, including the opportunity for non-traditional politicians and non-members of entrenched political dynasties to get elected.

But while some old dynasties went down with the Marcoses, the revolutionary government of Cory Aquino only gave rise to new dynasties. For example, the Binays replaced the Yabuts of Makati, the Revillas, Maliksis and Abayas replaced the Montanos in Cavite, the Belmontes replaced the Amorantos and Mathays, the Garcias replaced the Osmenas and Duranos in Cebu, etc.

Since then, moves have been made to implement Article II Section 26 of the 1987 Constitution that states: "The State shall guarantee equal access to opportunities for public service, and prohibit political dynasties as may be defined by law." Three bills have been filed in the House of Representatives that have since been consolidated into one (HB 3587) in December 2013. The bill applies the definition of political dynasty only if the number of elective officials from the same family is at least three. In short, only two relatives can be in elective offices at the same time.

The Senate bill (SB 2469, filed by Senator Miriam Defensor-Santiago in 2011, is more restrictive, allowing only one member of the family to hold office at any given time.

Both versions prohibit the immediate succession of a candidate related within second degree of consanguinity to an incumbent. Both, however, aim to control — rather than abolish — political dynasties.

While it is also unfair to prohibit a relative of a sitting elected official to run for office especially if he or she is competent, there is a need to somewhat control these political families from further expanding their reach and solidifying their hold on their jurisdiction.

In the interest of democracy and to allow more people to be given the opportunity to serve in an elective position, Congress will have to do its task of defining the parameters of political dynasty as embodied in the Constitution.

It is close to improbable that Congress would pass an anti-political dynasty bill considering that 70% of them are themselves members of such dynasties, but the people must continue to put the pressure on our legislators because the sooner these political clans are disempowered, the closer the country would be to achieving social justice and inclusive economic growth.

Ooooo

12

In praise of the Supreme Court

March 24, 2016

WHEN President Aquino appointed Maria Lourdes Sereno as Chief Justice of the Supreme Court shortly after successfully impeaching Chief Justice Renato Corona in August 2012, I must admit I had some reservations about her competence and independence.

Of course, she had impeccable credentials, having graduated as valedictorian of her class at the University of the Philippines College of Law in 1984 and having earned a Master of Laws degree from the University of Michigan Law School nine years later. But she had only served two years in the high tribunal, being the first appointee of Aquino to the Supreme Court in 2010. Before her appointment to the SC, she didn't have any bench experience. And the other associate justices had even more impressive credentials, more experience and seniority than the then 52-year-old justice.

When Aquino bypassed all the senior justices who were mostly appointed by President Gloria Macapagal Arroyo, it wasn't a surprise that many people, including this writer, saw it as an unclouded attempt by Aquino to control the judiciary as tightly as he controlled the legislative branch. Coming as it did just after Aquino had masterminded Corona's impeachment, doubts were raised on Sereno's impartiality. Will she allow herself to be used by Aquino in his frequent fights with Congress and to silence his critics?

Many feared that her appointment would create a crisis in the judiciary. In fact, eight of the other 13 justices snubbed her inauguration in protest over Aquino's refusal to follow the long-revered seniority rule. But officials of the Integrated Bar of the Philippines were willing to give her the benefit of the doubt. After all, she landed second in a mock election among 24 IBP officers for the Chief Justice post because she "had very clear and very concrete proposals to reform the judiciary."

The Makati Business Club was even more supportive. It hailed Sereno's selection as the 24th Chief Justice, the second youngest, and the first woman to head the judiciary. "We believe that the President has chosen a morally upright person with impeccable integrity, independence of mind, and competence essential for the highest magistrate of the land," the MBC said.

"The impeachment trial of former Chief Justice Renato Corona divided the country and greatly tested the faith of the people in our justice system. We sincerely hope that our new Chief Justice rebuilds the people's trust in the institution by ensuring greater transparency and accountability in the courts," the MBC added.

Apparently, Sereno has succeeded in bringing back the trust of the people, if not in the entire judiciary, at least in the Supreme Court. In the last two surveys conducted by Pulse Asia, the Supreme Court scored a 51-percent approval rating in December 2015 and 45 percent this month. These scores beat both houses of Congress by a mile and also that of Aquino who got an approval rating of only 38 percent, his lowest ever.

There are big reasons for people to trust again the Supreme Court after Aquino almost totally destroyed it by picking on the high tribunal at every turn since he orchestrated the impeachment of its Chief Justice in 2012. Aquino's confrontation with the tribunal peaked following the court's two decisions that declared the Priority Development Assistance Fund (PDAF or the congressional pork) unconstitutional in 2013 and the Disbursement Acceleration Program (DAP) as illegal in 2014.

The two unanimous rulings against the pork barrel (14-0 against PDAF and 13-0 against DAP) were not the only reasons the Supreme Court has won back the people's trust.

For example, last November, the tribunal abandoned the condonation doctrine on the case of the Ombudsman's preventive suspension against now dismissed Makati Mayor Jejomar Erwin Binay Jr. over alleged anomaly in the Makati City Hall Building 2 project. The younger Binay invoked the doctrine, which effectively extinguishes a reelected official's administrative liability from wrongdoing during a previous term, but the high court upheld Binay's suspension.

Earlier in August, the tribunal, citing humanitarian reasons, granted bail to opposition stalwart Sen. Juan Ponce Enrile, I'm sure to the consternation of Aquino.

In October, the high court again went against the wishes of Aquino when it granted relief to former President and now Pampanga Rep. Gloria Macapagal-Arroyo in her plunder case before the Sandiganbayan with a 30-day status quo ante order halting the trial proceedings involving the alleged P366-million Philippine Charity Sweepstakes Office (PCSO) fund anomaly. After the 30-day period lapsed, the SC extended the status quo ante order for another 60 days and when it lapsed again last Feb.16, the court ordered another 60-day trial suspension.

This was in addition to several furloughs the high court granted to Arroyo to spend Christmas and New Year in her La Vista home and another five days for her coming birthday.

And there were more rulings that showed the independence and efficiency of the Sereno-led Supreme Court:

• In June 2015, the tribunal stopped the implementation of two executive orders of President Aquino authorizing the privatization and utilization of coconut levy funds amounting to some P73.4 billion by the government.

• In September 2015, the tribunal ordered the government to compensate the Philippine International Air Terminals Co. Inc. (Piatco) at least $510 million for the expropriation of the Ninoy Aquino International Airport Terminal 3.

• In January, the tribunal ruled that the Enhanced Defense Cooperation Agreement (EDCA) between the Philippines and the United States (US) is constitutional.

• Also in January, the tribunal ordered the House of Representatives to oust sitting Marinduque Rep. Regina Ongsiako-Reyes and replace her with Lord Allan Jay Velasco, the runnerup in the 2013 congressional race.

• In February, the tribunal validated with finality the 2013 election of Antique Gov. Exequiel Javier as it junked the motion for reconsideration of Javier's political adversaries pressing for his disqualification over the issue of his having suspended a local official during an election period.

• Early this month, the tribunal reminded judges of lower courts to be careful in issuing warrants of arrest and search warrants so as not to violate constitutional rights and judicial procedures.

• Also this month, the tribunal cleared the way for Sen. Grace Poe to run for President, voting to reverse the Commission on Elections (Comelec) orders disqualifying her for not meeting citizenship and residency requirements.

• On March 7, voting 14-0, the tribunal ordered the Commission on Elections to issue ballot receipts during the May 9 polls. On May 16, the tribunal junked the poll body's reconsideration plea just 30 minutes after terminating oral arguments on the case.

Probably alarmed by the rising number of judicial defeats by the administration, Aquino last Monday called the Supreme Court to review controversial cases and look into judicial processes hampering the speedy implementation of the government's infrastructure projects.

"The truth is, you are the experts in law and my appeal is: Review serious and controversial issues faced by the judiciary, like the times when the position of one or a few justices became suspicious, when the Supreme Court's position on important issues changed, or when judicial legislation seemed to have occurred," Aquino said in a speech during the groundbreaking of the future site of the SC complex in Fort Bonifacio, Taguig City.

He said a new building could help them become more efficient, but it would still be up to them if they would push for what was right and just. The head of the Executive Branch is basically telling its co-equal Judicial Branch, "I am giving you a new building and new equipment, so perhaps you should be more accommodating to us."

Although spoken in a milder manner, the President's remarks remind us of his virulent criticism of the Supreme Court the day after the adverse DAP ruling. He said: "My message to the Supreme Court: we don't want to get to a point where two co-equal branches of government would clash and where a third branch would have to mediate," Aquino said. "There was something that you did in the past, which you tried to do again, and there are those who are saying that [the DAP decision] is worse."

With the impartiality and hard work shown by the 14 justices, led by Chief Justice Sereno, in its recent high-profile decisions, I am certain that the high court will continue to resist pressures from both Malacanang and Congress and maintain its independence as the final arbiter of judicial issues.

Ooooo

13
SC must not bow to Comelec threats
March 17, 2016

SOMETHING is very wrong with the Philippines' Commission on Elections. After failing to submit its comment to a petition by former Senator Richard J. Gordon to compel the Comelec to issue receipts to voters after casting their votes in the May 9 polls, it now blames the tribunal for not giving them a chance to give its side.

Instead of submitting their reply to the petition as ordered by the court, the Comelec lawyers asked for a five-day extension. But the tribunal wouldn't have any of their delaying tactics. After all, the election is less than two months away. The poll commissioners had ruled unanimously, 7-0, against Gordon's petition and it shouldn't be too hard for them to give their side if they indeed discussed the petition lengthily before making that unanimous ruling.

And so the Supreme Court, also unanimously (14-0), reversed the Comelec ruling and ordered the poll body to activate the Voter Verification Paper Audit Trail (VVPAT) component of the automated poll counting machine, which gives voting receipts to voters after they had cast their vote.

The Comelec didn't stop in blaming the Supreme Court for not granting it a five-day extension to air their side. The poll body appealed for reconsideration and now Comelec Chairman Andres Bautista warns everybody that if the May 9 election fails, it is the result of the SC decision's decision ordering the poll body to issue voter receipts.

And now, he says, the Comelec may have to move the elections to June 9 and also warns that chaos might ensue if it is unable to declare any winners by June 30, when the terms of incumbent officials end. Bautista says the Comelec may also be forced to shift to manual voting if it cannot postpone the polls by one month.

Why Bautista would even suggest a return to manula voting when the law clearly mandades poll automation in elections, including the May 9 polls, is beyond me. Do the election commissioners even understand or respect the law?

The Comelec is basically resorting to blackmail by putting the pressure on the tribunal to reverse its decision.

I don't think the Supreme Court would reverse its unanimous decision based on these virtual threats from the Comelec. After all, the law is very clear on the need to activate the VVPAT.

Gordon points out that under Section 7 (e) of Republic Act 9369 or the Automated Election Law, the VVPAT is one of the required minimum systems capabilities of the automated election system and a major security feature of the vote counting machine. He should know because he is the principal author of the law.

Twice, the Comelec did not implement this provision, during the first automated election in 2010 and again in the senatorial and local elections in 2013. In the 2010 presidential elections, it used the discredited Precinct Count Optical Scan machines minus the paper audit trail. In 2013, it used the same PCOS machines also without the VVPAT.

And in the coming May elections, Comelec had again decided against using the VVPAT because, Bautista said, it could be used as a tool for vote buying and would also extend the voting period by seven hours. But it has been almost nine years since Automated Election Law was passed in 2007. Surely, the Comelec could have come out by now with a reliable system to implement its provision on the voting receipts.

It would seem that there never was any effort by the Comelec to enforce the VVPAT provision, which, according to Gordon, allows every voter to confirm whether or not the machine cast the vote correctly based on the choice of the voter, thereby ensuring the integrity of the elections.

"Several safeguards were put in place to ensure the sanctity of the ballot. Among these safeguards was the VVPAT. A voter verified paper audit trail consists of physical paper records of voter ballots as voters have cast them on an electronic voting system. The voter-verified part refers to the fact that the voter is given the opportunity to verify that the choices indicated on the paper record correspond to the choices that the voter has made in casting the ballot," Gordon said in his petition.

Gordon added that the VVPAT serves as a deterrent against election fraud and provides a means to audit stored electronic result. He added that Sections 6(e), (f) and (n) of the said law is clear and unequivocal in mandating the use of the VVPAT and that it is not up to the Comelec whether or not to implement it.

By refusing to give voting receipts, the Comelec has violated the law twice already – in 2010 and in 2013. And now, it wants Supreme Court approval to violate it one more time.

The Comelec must not be allowed to violate the law again. Gordon correctly pointed out that its refusal to activate the VVPAT is one of the reasons why there are those who have questioned the credibility of the automated election system, in addition to the failure of the poll body to implement other safeguards, such as presenting the source code for review and disabling the use of digital signatures.

The Supreme Court must not give in to warnings of election failure scenarios being dangled by the Comelec. The Comelec commissioners should not be allowed to pressure the Supreme Court to allow them to do what it is convenient for them or whatever they choose to do. The law is very clear and it's about time the Comelec does its duties correctly.

The Comelec commissioners cannot fall back on their excuse that it's running out of time. Why then did they not activate and test it earlier? What law gave them the authority to decide that the VVPAT should not be implemented because it can be used for vote buying? Are they just too lazy and incompetent to implement that law to the letter, or are they intentionally leaving room for a fraud much bigger than vote buying?

Bayan Muna party-list Rep. Carlos Zarate said the Comelec's actions are a disgrace and only bolster public distrust in the election process. The issue of voter receipts is not new, in fact, and has been raised since 2010, he added.

"If only Comelec did not choose to be blind, deaf and numb to the demands and proposals for a more transparent process, it could have inspired more confidence in the upcoming elections," he said.

Instead, the Comelec is now holding the nation hostage with its threats of a failed election.

Ooooo

14

Why Duterte and Marcos are contenders

March 9, 2016

IT IS a source of wonder why 30 years after Filipinos staged a peaceful revolt to oust a dictator, many of them now seem eager or willing to embrace a presidential candidate who threatens to impose a strongman rule and a vice presidential aspirant who is the namesake son of the supposedly hated leader they deposed in what is now known as People Power Revolution.

If the surveys were to be believed, it seems Davao City Mayor Rodrigo Duterte, who admits to using strongman tactics to combat crime and corruption in his city and promises to do the same when elected, and Sen. Ferdinand "Bongbong" Marcos Jr., who firmly believes the country was on the road to greatness until the EDSA uprising stopped short his father's term in 1986, have a greater than fighting chance of being elected president and vice president, respectively, in the May 9 elections.

President Aquino and the ruling Liberal Party have moved heaven and earth to destroy Duterte and Marcos as they did — also unsuccessfully it seems — to bring down Vice President Jejomar Binay ahead of the May 9 elections and hopefully boost the chances of their candidates, Mar Roxas and Rep. Leni Robredo .

In the latest Pulse Asia survey released last Friday, Binay and Sen. Grace Poe and Vice President Jejomar Binay were statistically tied for top spot in the presidential preference poll with 26 percent each, while Duterte and Roxas were also tied with 21 percent. Sen. Miriam Defensor-Santiago was in last place with three percent.

In the same survey, Marcos and Sen. Francis "Chiz" Escudero are now statistically tied in the vice presidential race. Escudero had 29 percent of the respondents, while Marcos had 26 percent. In third place was Robredo with 19 percent. Sen. Alan Peter Cayetano was in fourth with 12 percent, followed by Sen. Antonio Trillanes with 6 percent, and Sen. Gringo Honasan, 4 percent.

In the latest survey conducted by The Standard in-house pollster published on Monday, Duterte (24 percent) edged closer to Poe (26 percent) while overtaking Binay (23 percent) and staying ahead of Roxas (22 percent).

In the vice presidential race, The Standard poll showed Escudero maintaining a six-point lead over Marcos. Escudero led with 30 percent, followed by Marcos (24 percent), Camarines Sur Rep. Leni Robredo (20 percent), Senator Alan Cayetano (11 percent), Senator Antonio Trillanes IV (seven percent) and Senator Gringo Honasan (4 percent).

These surveys confirm what many expected, that this election is shaping up to be the closest and toughest presidential race in the country's history. As they say in basketball, there have been many lead changes and ties, ensuring a tightly fought finish.

While Binay, Poe and Escudero have been expected to be on top most of the way, the rise of Duterte and Marcos in the latest polls were surprising to many. The two surveys were conducted just before and after the 30th anniversary celebration of the EDSA People Power Revolt, and one would surmise that with the people being constantly reminded of the perils of strongman rule as exemplified by the martial law years, the appeal of Duterte and Marcos would diminish. Instead, their stars shone even more brightly.

I am surprised to this day that many people, even from the so-called civil society, are supporting either Duterte or Binay for president and Marcos for vice president. I know many doctors, lawyers, journalists and other professionals who swear to high heavens that Duterte is the kind of leader the country needs. Another group swears Marcos could make this country "great again." And others believe that despite all the graft cases against him, Binay is the one who could lift the masses from poverty.

One explanation is that some or many of the people who gathered on EDSA from Feb. 22 to 25, 1986 have been utterly disappointed that another set of oligarchs and dirty politicians have taken over the reins of the country and have not brought the hopes and aspirations of EDSA to reality. Thirty years later, the government is back to "business as usual" and the poor and the middle class remain ignored and forgotten.

Another explanation is that those who went to EDSA did not really reflect the general sentiment throughout the country at that time, and now the people outside of EDSA want to be heard this time.

As for Binay's continued stay on top despite the graft allegations, the poor have an explanation for it: "Pare-pareho lang namang corrupt yang mga yan, di doon na tayo sa malalapitan natin" or something to that effect. In other words, the masses are tired of politicians' pretensions of being honest and sincere while they and/or their cronies rob them dry. And that is bad because it seems the people have accepted corruption as a fact of life in the Philippines.

As I have said earlier, if this coming election were a referendum on whether the people believe Aquino's "daang matuwid" has succeeded in reforming the government and society in general, it would seem that based on the surveys, he is in for a resounding defeat.

We can go on and speculate but in the end, it is only the outcome of the May 9 elections that will ultimately matter in the next six years – whether the country could move forward or take a few more years backwards. And sans any election fraud, the people themselves will decide on which course the country would take.

Ooooo

15
Questions for bets on sea row
March 3, 2016

I AGREE completely with Supreme Court Associate Justice Antonio Carpio that the five presidential candidates should make known their stand in the ongoing dispute between the Philippines and China over several islands and reefs in the South China Sea.

Carpio said at a public lecture last week that the candidates must lay down their plan for the territorial dispute, which, he said, threatens not just the country's borders but also its fisheries, oil reserves and other critical resources within its exclusive economic zone (EEZ).

"If they are elected and they become President, and if this case is not yet decided, are they going to continue with the arbitration or withdraw the arbitration?" Carpio said. "If elected President, are they going to enter into joint development with China? Because the condition of China for joint development is [that] we concede sovereignty to them and they will give us 50 percent of resources within our EEZ."

I asked similar questions in an article in this corner in May last year ("Sea row: Where do the candidates stand?"):

"Will they stand with China in resolving the territorial disputes through bilateral talks? Will they continue Aquino's hardline stance against China on the dispute? Will they collaborate with China in anticipation of China's rise as an economic and military superpower? Or will they continue to align with the US in the looming battle for supremacy in the region? Are they ready to embrace the US's return to the Philippines in exchange for its support and protection? How do they intend to resolve the conflict without bringing the country to war?

At that time, only Vice President Jojo Binay of the United Nationalist Alliance (UNA) had made clear his stand. I wrote then:

"Vice President Jejomar Binay, who continues to lead presidential surveys albeit with narrowing margin, has already revealed his stand on the issue in a recent interview when he said that if he were elected president, he would support China's call for "bilateral talks" between the two countries over their territorial disputes and that he favored "joint ventures" with China.

"This stand would significantly soften the current Philippine policy towards China on the issue, and would be a repeat of Gloria Macapagal Arroyo's misadventures with China.

"Binay has clearly defined his stand on the issue. All the other candidates should reveal the strategy they intend to pursue in dealing with China regarding the territorial disputes. The voters have the right to know where the candidates stand on this very important issue."

The other candidates have since revealed their stands on the raging issue through the Philippine Daily Inquirer's series on the presidential bets. In that article ("Agenda of the next president: Foreign policy"), Binay reiterated his openness to a bilateral dialogue with China, but somehow took the middle stand by adding that he would "pursue all other legal options to promote our sovereign rights."

He said: "A Binay presidency will be firm in upholding our national interest while promoting a constructive bilateral dialogue with other countries such as China. At the same time, it will also pursue all other legal options to promote our sovereign rights, including continued consultation with and securing the support of the international community and our allies. Most of the disputed areas are in international waters and, therefore, keeping air and sea lanes open will not be a concern for the Philippines alone but for the international community as well. By having this common interest, countries, including China, will need to resolve disputes through dialogue and the rule of international law."

Former Interior and Local Government Secretary Mar Roxas, the administration and Liberal Party candidate, expectedly said he would continue "to pursue our claims at the United Nations. Our progress in the arbitration case in the International Tribunal on the Laws of the Seas (ITLOS) signifies our commitment to the rule of law—whoever you are, whatever your country is, in the eyes of the law, we are all equal."

Roxas also said the country would, at the same time, work with other nations to come up with a Binding Code of Conduct for the South China Sea. In the same breath, however, Roxas made sure not to antagonize China as he said: "But we also recognize that this issue is not the totality of our relations with China. At the end of the day, we want to achieve stability, which is in the interest of all parties involved. Without stability, we can't have long-lasting prosperity. Otherwise, our country's economic resurgence will always be under threat."

Sen. Grace Poe did not offer specific plans, but said in general terms that her administration would "adhere to international law in settling disputes with other countries and seek alliances with those who share the same values." She added that the Philippines must assume a leadership role in Asean, and "strengthen our international bargaining power by nurturing a stronger, more relevant economy with a modern armed forces."

Davao City Mayor Rodrigo Duterte, like Binay, said he will be "open to dialogue with

China but with the involvement of Asean since the dispute covers several countries with similar interests to the Philippines. While our legitimate claim initiated at the United Nations will proceed, we need to engage in peaceful dialogue as well." Unlike Binay, though, Duterte is in favor of a multilateral dialogue, which would involve all claimants and the Asean, which is also the stand of the Aquino administration.

The fifth candidate, Sen. Miriam Defensor Santiago, said: "I will adopt a second level of diplomacy with regard to the West Philippine Sea dispute, as the other party takes keen interest in bilateral negotiation bordering on conciliation, relying apparently on the principles set forth in the UNCLOS, Part 15, Section 1. It is not true at all that the Arbitral Tribunal of UNCLOS, Annex 7, may decide on the Philippine side in the face of China's excepting itself from the application of Articles 297 and 298 of the UNCLOS."

If my interpretation is right, Santiago favors a bilateral dialogue with China just like Binay and her running mate, Sen. Bongbong Marcos.

I hope that the moderators in the next presidential debate will ask pertinent questions on the territorial dispute with China so that the voters would have a clearer picture on how they stand on the burning issue.

The Department of Foreign Affairs, said it expects a decision by the International Arbitration Tribunal on the Philippine case against China by May. That would be around the time of the election and before the next president assumes position on June 30, 2016.

This early, the people have the right to know what the five candidates would do in case the Philippines won the case. How does he or she intend to make China abide by the arbitration decision, knowing that China, which has refused to participate in the proceedings, has clearly stated that it would not abide by any decision of the tribunal? If elected, will that candidate use the legal victory as leverage and sit down for a bilateral dialogue with China?"

If in the remote possibility that the tribunal decides against the Philippines, how will the next president proceed? Will he just give up sovereignty to China?

If the tribunal bides for more time to make its decision, what will the candidate do if he is elected president?

These and other related questions need answers from those who wish to become president in 2016. And we need them now before we decide on whom to vote.

Ooooo

16
Tensions rise in South China Sea
February 25, 2016

LESS than two weeks ago, Russian Prime Minister Dmitry Medvedev warned of a new Cold War between East and West as it accused the

North Atlantic Treaty Organization (NATO) of being "hostile and closed" towards Russia.

While a Cold War between Russia, on one side, and the United States and NATO member countries, on the other, still has to unfold, it would seem that a Cold War between the US and some Asian countries, on one hand, and China, on the other, has actually begun.

China's aggressive stance in the South China Sea and the US' recent moves to hasten its "Pivot to Asia" policy are leading to an escalated militarization of the region. Both China and the US have accused each other of militarizing the South China Sea.

Last week, US Secretary of State John Kerry slammed China for its increased "militarization" in the South China Sea after Taiwan said Beijing placed surface-to-air missiles on a disputed island there.

"There is every evidence, every day, that there has been an increase of militarization of one kind or another. It's of a serious concern," Kerry told reporters.

China, on the other hand, said it was the US that's militarizing the South China Sea. Chinese Foreign Ministry spokesman Hong Lei told reporters that patrols by US military aircraft and Navy vessels, along with joint exercises involving regional partners, were the true reason why concerns were growing over peace and stability in the region.

"The above actions have escalated tensions in the South China Sea, and that's the real militarization of the South China Sea," Hong said.

The past week's exchange of accusations by both sides followed reports, confirmed by satellite images and neither denied or confirmed by Chinese authorities, that China installed several surface-to-air missile launchers and a radar system on Woody Island, a part of the Paracels island group that China has controlled since a bloody battle with Vietnamese troops in 1974 that in the death of 54 Viet soldiers.

Experts say the missiles could be used to target enemy aircraft. HIS Jane's Intelligence Review deputy editor Neil Ashdown said that depending on the version of the HQ-9 deployed, the system has a range of between 125 km and 230 km, and would be the most advanced surface-to-air missile system currently deployed on land in the South China Sea. Ashdown described that as a significant military escalation.

China's Ministry of Defense confirmed that "China has deployed weapons on the island for a long time", but did not specify which weapons were on the island.

The ministry attempted to downplay the deployment, saying "China has the fair and legal right to deploy defense facilities within the boundaries of its own territory."

Reports of the installation of missile launchers and radar system on the disputed island came only one day after US President Barack Obama met with leaders of the 10-member Association of Southeast Asian Nations (ASEAN) in Rancho Mirage, California. The satellite launchers were apparently installed while the summit was going on, an arrogant gesture meant to challenge US power and influence in the region.

The military escalation also came a few days after a ministerial dialogue in Washington DC among Foreign Affairs Secretary Albert del Rosario and Defense Secretary Voltaire T. Gazmin of the Philippines and Secretary of State John Kerry and Secretary of Defense Ash Carter of the US, after which the four officials issued a joint statement that highlighted the importance of parties taking active steps to reduce tensions, including halting the reclamation, construction on, and militarization of outposts in the South China Sea and to refrain from any actions that harass, coerce, or intimidate other parties in the South China Sea.

Tensions in the sea — through which one-third of global trade worth $5 trillion passes every year — have mounted in recent months since China transformed contested reefs in the Spratly islands into artificial islands capable of supporting military facilities.

Earlier, the US and China already traded warnings and accusations after China conducted test flights on its newly constructed airstrips on Fiery Cross (Kagitingan island), which the Philippines claims is part of the Kalayaan island group.

State Department spokesman John Kirby reiterated a US call for a halt to land reclamation and militarization of outposts in the South China Sea, saying that to begin flight operations at this new airfield in a disputed area raises tensions and threatens regional stability."

The Philippines and Vietnam, which both claim Fiery Cross along with other islands and reefs in the area, protested the reef landings as threats to regional stability and were joined by Japan, which has its own territorial disputes with China.

The US has been very busy consolidating its power and influence in the region in recent weeks. It has invited Asian leaders to Washington, conducted the PH-US ministerial dialogues, invited Asean journalists to briefings by American military officials in Honolulu, base of the US Pacific Fleet; expanded its war exercises with its Asian allies, and has continued to test China's resolve by ordering its military planes and warships to fly or sail close to the islands where China has built military installations.

The tensions have started an arms race in Asia, with Vietnam vigorously pursuing a military acquisition and modernization program that includes the purchase of six new submarines and the Philippines slowly beefing its military capability with new patrol boats and helicopters. In addition, the Philippines is allowing the use of eight military bases by American forces and vessels under the Supreme Court-upheld Enhanced Defense Cooperation Agreement (EDCA).

Washington is also deploying more Patriot missiles in South Korea, which would enhance defense not only against North Korean missiles but also against Chinese missiles. Taiwan and Japan are also beefing up their forces.

China, apparently in a rush to become a legitimate military power, spent in excess of $145 billion last year as it advanced a program modernizing an arsenal of drones, warships, jets, missiles and cyber weapons.

At present, China has close to 2,800 military aircrafts. China is also expanding its navy, with the acquisition of one aircraft carrier and the construction of four more in the coming years. It also has 45 frigates, 24 destroyers, 69 submarines and 353 coastal defense crafts. It has the biggest army with more than two million active troops and more than two million more active reserves.

Ian Storey, a senior fellow and specialist in regional maritime security issues at the Iseas-Yusof Ishak Institute in Singapore, said: "What we have seen over the past few weeks has become the new normal. Tensions ebb and flow in the South China Sea and... I suspect it could get worse mainly because of these facilities on the reclaimed islands which are being operationalized."

He added: "China is building three airstrips; my guess is they will become operational within the next few months. That means China will be able to exert a bigger presence... and that is likely to raise tensions and lead to more incidents."

There is no doubt that tensions have built up significantly in the South China Sea, making it a major flashpoint in the world, and with the US responding more aggressively to the China threat, the new Cold War can easily escalate and place Asia – and consequently, the entire world – in the precipice of war.

This situation makes it even more important for us Filipinos to seriously study the emotional conditions and foreign policy programs of the presidential candidates in both the Philippines and the United States, which are holding presidential elections this year.

The new leaders will be faced with tough decisions on what to do with the powder keg that's floating on the South China Sea. Such decisions can mean prolonged peace or accelerated war.

Ooooo

17
Surveys should alarm Aquino
February 18, 2016

THE LATEST surveys of Pulse Asia and the Social Weather Station confirmed what many have predicted all along – the May 9 presidential elections will be the closest race in the history of the Philippines. The surveys also seem to ensure that the next president will become another minority president, just as all the elected presidents in the post-Marcos era had been.

The coming presidential poll promises to be even tighter than the 2004 presidential elections when incumbent Gloria Macapagal Arroyo defeated actor Fernando Poe Jr by the narrowest of margins – a mere 3.48 percent or

1,123,576 votes – for the presidency, and broadcaster Noli de Castro bested fellow broadcaster Sen. Loren Legarda by only 2.9 percent.

The 2004 elections became so controversial following the "Hello Garci" scandal that revealed a phone conversation between Arroyo and Comelec Commissioner Virgilio Garcillano where the president allegedly asked the poll official to rig the elections. Arroyo was nearly toppled in July that year in the midst of massive street protests that followed the Garci scandal.

Poe filed an electoral protest but died of heart attack before the case could be adjudicated.

The 1992 elections was almost just as close with former Defense Secretary Fidel V. Ramos becoming the first president elected under the 1987 Constitution with a margin of only 3.86 percent or 874,348 votes – a mere 23.58% of the vote against Sen. Miriam Defensor Santiago (19.72%), businessman Danding Cojuangco (18.17%), former Speaker Ramon Mitra (14.64%), former First Lady Imelda Romualdez Marcos (10.32%), former Senate President Jovito Salonga (10.16%) and former Vice President Doy Laurel (3.4%).

The 1992 race was so close, Santiago, who led in the first five days of canvassing, immediately filed an electoral protest that has since been dismissed.

The May elections could do a repeat of these two close contests, hopefully without any claims of cheating.

The Pulse Asia survey showed that Sen. Grace Poe had regained her lead to become the leading candidate in 2016. The survey, which was conducted from January 24 to 28, revealed that 30 percent of the respondents would vote for Poe. Vice President Jejomar Binay got 23 percent, while Liberal Party standard-bearer Manuel "Mar" Roxas II and Davao City Mayor Rodrigo "Rody" Duterte both garnered 20 percent.

In the SWS survey, which was conducted in the first week of February, Binay was back on top with 29 percent, with Duterte and Poe tied in second place with 24 percent. Roxas had 18 percent, while Sen. Miriam Defensor-Santiago got 4 percent.

It has been a roller coaster rides in the last few months for the candidates except for Roxas, who is climbing steadily but excruciatingly slowly, and Santiago, whose failing health has prevented her from conducting a more aggressive campaign. Binay, Poe and Duterte had taken the lead at one time or another in the last few months, which was caused more by the uncertainty of the outcome of the disqualification cases against Poe and Duterte rather than by the candidates' platform or the efficiency of their campaigns.

No definite pattern could be established by the surveys until the disqualification cases against Poe and Duterte are resolved with finality by the Supreme Court. This situation makes it even more urgent for the Tribunal to decide on the cases at the soonest possible time.

However, the surveys of the past several months have established for certain that Binay, despite a slew of allegations of corruption against him, is the man to beat in May. The Makati mayor has withstood all damaging allegations against him and his family and has kept his core base of about 23 to 25 percent through all the surveys.

Very close behind is Poe, who started strongly since she announced her candidacy in September, toppling Binay until questions on her qualification surfaced a few weeks later. Poe has also stayed above the 23-percent level even after the Comelec disqualified her in December, the appeal of which remains pending in the Supreme Court.

If the surveys were to be believed, it will be a very close fight among Binay, Poe and Duterte unless the Davao mayor runs himself out of the race with his reckless pronouncements or simply runs out of cash before May 9.

The LP hierarchy remains optimistic that Roxas can still catch up with the three leading contenders. Senate President Franklin Drilon is confident that Roxas' numbers would further improve before election day since the administration has the "biggest political machinery" and has the "most credible campaign manager" in the person of President Aquino himself.

"And therefore, we're confident that over the next three months, we'd be able to bring the numbers of Mar Roxas and Leni Robredo especially that were standing on the platform of 'daang-matuwid' (straight path)," he said.

But some political observers, including this writer, believe that it is precisely the fact that Roxas does not offer anything new, but only promises to continue Aquino's "daang matuwid" that keeps him shackled to the bottom of the heap. Voters have expressed doubts on Aquino's reform agenda as shown by his continuously dipping approval ratings, which dropped below 50% for the first time last week, and as shown by the continued popularity of Binay, who the administration has alleged to be the anti-thesis of the "daang matuwid."

Aquino has joined Roxas in his campaign rallies lately, but the Capiz politician remains lagging behind the three leading candidates with less than three months left before the May 9 polls.

Another indication of the voters' dissatisfaction of the way the government has been run since the time of Aquino's mother, the late President Cory Aquino, until her son's term is the steady rise of Sen. Bongbong Marcos, the only son and namesake of the late strongman Ferdinand Marcos, in the vice presidential surveys.

Marcos, who has been the target of Malacanang's missiles lately, has caught up with popular Sen. Chiz Escudero, who has led the vice presidential surveys since Day One, in the latest SWs survey. The two young senators have 26 percent each, ahead of Aquino's candidate, Rep. Leni Robredo, who has 19 percent; and Duterte's running mate, Sen. Alan Cayetano, with 16 percent.

If indeed the May 9 election is a referendum on the success of the Aquino administration, it seems, according to surveys, that it is facing a resounding rebuff.

Ooooo

18
Time to end cycle of migration
February 11, 2016

THE government is bracing for a conceivably crippling crisis involving the possible layoff of some 1.5 million overseas Filipino workers (OFWs) currently employed as temporary workers in the Middle East because of the precipitous slide in world oil prices in the recent weeks.

These temporary workers account for about 75% of the more than 2 million OFWs in the region. President Aquino, according to Malacanang spokesmen, has ordered the Department of Labor to prepare measures to soften the impact of the impending job losses.

Communications Secretary Sonny Coloma hailed his boss as being "pro-active" on the situation, saying that the President is acting on the problem although "there is no indication yet that it is happening."

I can't see how acting while the country is about to fall on the precipice can be considered "pro-active." The President is, in fact, merely reacting to an almost certain crisis. If he were a "pro-active" President, Aquino should have on his first year in office instructed his labor and economic managers to prepare an exit plan from the country's dependence on foreign labor deployment, knowing fully well that doing so could spell trouble for the country's economy and population.

While the Migrante International, which is tracking OFW developments all over the world, has warned of the stark possibility of the massive job losses in the Middle East, Labor Secretary Rosalinda Baldoz remains optimistic and says that massive retrenchment of OFWs in the Middle East is "far from happening."

Baldoz pointed to the latest data from the DOLE's field offices in the Middle East showing that job losses for the January reporting period had so far been either negligible or altogether non-existent. In the eastern Saudi region (where the bulk of its oil industry is based), labor officials reported a 1.1-percent decrease in job orders or employment contracts processed between December 2015 and January 2016.

She reports a continued decrease in job orders in other places in the region, but she describes it as "negligible." She said the job losses can be attributed more to the "Saudization" of the labor force rather than the glut in global oil supply that has resulted in the sudden drop of world oil prices.

Oil prices have sunk to below $30 a barrel, the lowest level in 12 years, before making a slight recovery amid a glut due to additional supply in the United States, refusal of the Oil Petroleum Exporting Countries to cut production and the economic slowdown in China. The end of Western sanctions on Iran is expected to worsen the glut.

Since the middle of 2014, the price of a barrel of crude has fallen more than 70 percent.

Because of the prolonged price slump, Saudi Arabia, the world's biggest oil exporter, suffered a budget deficit of about $100 billion in 2015, forcing it to cut subsidies and scale down public projects. Other oil exporters in the Middle East are in similar straits.

These can only mean an economic slowdown in the region, which, in turn, could easily translate to less demand for workers not only in the oil industry, but also in a broad spectrum of businesses, including construction where the bulk of Filipino workers are employed outside of the oil industry.

And yet, the Aquino administration seems optimistic that those to be displaced can easily find jobs that are currently available in the country. Maybe if only 50,000 were to be displaced, but what if even just half of the 1.5 million temporary workers in the Middle East were laid off?

Where will all these 750,000 suddenly unemployed Filipinos find jobs? How will they support their families? Can you imagine that many people suddenly returning to the country and laying idle for months, or possibly years?

The Aquino administration, which has benefitted from the ever-increasing money remittances of the close to 12 million Filipino workers abroad, has opted to continue sending thousands of Filipinos abroad instead of finding ways to achieve "inclusive growth" that would stop the cycle of migration in the country.

The overseas Filipino workers program was initiated by then Labor Secretary Blas F. Ople in the 1970s as a temporary remedy to the unemployment problem. Most countries transitioning from an agricultural-based economy to an industrialized one had to deploy workers abroad at one time or another. Taiwan and South Korea, for example, used to be two of the biggest exporters of labor. But with industrialization, their citizens now stay at home and travel only as tourists or businessmen.

The same is true with China and India, which are the world's two biggest labor exporters. They have transitioned to become two of the strongest economies in the world, and will soon be importing instead of exporting labor. The Philippines, which is the third biggest labor exporter, remains poor and unable to provide jobs to its population.

Unlad Kabayan, a non-profit based in the Philippines, said "There is a definite cycle of migration: Filipino workers go abroad, earn a little, return to the Philippines, use up the savings, and then work abroad again. The challenge is to break this cycle, and provide an alternative to migration."

Indeed, the government has to start refocusing its priorities to stop this "culture of migration" and keep its workers home, so that they don't have to suffer the indignities of working for foreigners and their children don't have to grow up without their parents.

But lulled into complacency by the sweet scent of the dollar, our leaders would rather keep the status quo, never mind what ills it would bring in the future.

During his campaign for the presidency, candidate Noynoy Aquino said of his vision on the issue of the OFWs: "From a government that treats its people as an export commodity and a means to earn foreign currency to a government that creates jobs at home so that working abroad will be a choice rather than a necessity; and when its citizens do choose to become OFWs, their welfare and protection will still be the government's priority."

Aquino even boasted in his last State-of-the-Nation Address (SONA) that the number of OFWs have been reduced due to improved local job generation.

But Migrante said that under the Aquino administration, the number of OFWs leaving the country increased due to chronic joblessness and low wages – from 2,500 daily before Aquino assumed office in 2009, to 4,018 in 2010, to 6,092 daily by early 2015 citing Department of Labor and Employment data.

Migrante added that Philippine Overseas Employment Administration (POEA) data showed that the Aquino government has breached the two million mark in OFW deployment processing in 2013, the highest record in the history of Philippine labor export.

Migrante agreed with Aquino that there has been a notable "reverse migration" from the Middle East, but it is not because the country has attained "inclusive growth" as claimed by Aquino, but because civil unrests, calamities, economic instabilities and other similar factors in migrant-receiving countries.

With the continuous repatriation of distressed OFWs from Saudi Arabia, Egypt, Syria and Libya, and the deportation of undocumented

OFWs from Europe, Canada and the United States, the government should start thinking "long-term" in addressing the problem.

Instead of staying in denial, the government should accept the fact that the Philippine economy can't depend on foreign remittances to maintain its growth. It should work on the premise that it has to provide jobs to stop the cycle of migration and maintain a stable and "inclusive" economic growth.

Ooooo

19
Is Poe Aquino's 'Manchurian candidate'?
February 3, 2016

SINCE the start of the year, Sen. Grace Poe has been getting unexpected support in the disqualification cases against her that are now pending before the Supreme Court.

In the first week of January, the independent presidential candidate got a totally unexpected support from the government's top lawyer, Solicitor General Florin Hilbay, who caught everybody by surprise when he asked the Supreme Court to uphold the Senate Electoral Tribunal (SET) decision that Poe is a natural-born Filipino citizen and was therefore qualified to run for senator in the 2013 elections.

Hilbay was basically saying Poe was also qualified to run for president when he said the SET reasonably and correctly ruled that proof of private respondent's status as a foundling did not necessarily equate to the lack of proof of Filipino parentage, adding that neither did it translate to an inability to prove Filipino parentage.

In his comment submitted to the high tribunal, Hilbay also said the minority opinion of the three SC justices in the electoral tribunal that Poe needs to prove that either of her biological parents is Filipino was an undue burden on the senator.

"To impose scientific levels of certainty, as by way of a DNA sample of a Filipino parent, as the only acceptable means to prove one's filiation, would be to impose a burden significantly higher than that which is normally required for these proceedings," he said.

Two weeks later, a similarly surprising support came from SC Justice Marvic Leonen who asked why a foundling like Poe would be compelled to look for her real parents or required to prove her parentage, such as through DNA testing, when ordinary Filipinos only need to show their birth certificates to prove their parentage and citizenship.

Leonen also agreed with the position of former Chief Justice Artemio Panganiban, who held that the expressed provision of the Constitution on qualifications of presidential aspirants should be disregarded and the issue thrown to the electorate, saying the voice of the people is the voice of God.

Chief Justice Ma. Lourdes Sereno said a few days later during the SC hearing that Philippine adoption laws recognize foundlings or children with no known parents as Filipino citizens, basically backing Poe's contention that she is a natural-born citizen qualified to run for president of the Philippines.

Zeroing in on who should carry the burden of proof that Poe is not a natural-born Filipino and hence not qualified to seek public office, Sereno said compelling a foundling to prove his or her unknown parentage was an "impossible condition," and that upholding such a requirement would betray the presumption in Philippine adoption laws that a foundling is a Filipino.

The supportive statements of three of the top legal minds in the country, without a doubt, raised the hopes of Poe and her supporters that the high tribunal would eventually rule that the foundling Poe is a natural-born citizen and, therefore, qualified to run as president of the country.

The views of Sereno, Leonen and Hilbay caught many by surprise because all three were appointees of President Aquino, who has publicly endorsed his party's presidential nominee, former Interior Secretary Mar Roxas.

It may be that the three are just playing out their role as impartial jurists regardless of who appointed them to their posts, but it doesn't help that their opinions came just after both Pulse Asia and Social Weather Station (SWS) surveys showed opposition candidate Vice President Jejomar Binay back on toop of the presidential race. Both surveys came amid speculations that the Comelec and the SC may disqualify Poe and Davao City Mayor Rodrigo Duterte, the other popular presidential aspirant.

It is not difficult to speculate that the surveys sent shivers on Aquino's spine. He and other LP leaders probably thought that disqualifying erstwhile frontrunners Poe and Duterte would help raise Roxas' ratings. But to their surprise, it was Binay who stood to benefit from the disqualification.

The mere thought that Binay could become the next president should be enough to give Aquino sleepless nights, knowing that the UNA candidate blames him for what he calls persecution of his family, not to mention that three opposition senators the administration had jailed for their alleged role in the Janet Napoles pork barrel scam – Senators Juan Ponce Enrile, Jinggoy Estrada and Bong Revilla – are Binay's supporters.

Thoughts of a Binay presidency conjures the possibility of detention for Aquino since the opposition has vowed to pursue criminal cases against him once his term is over and his presidential immunity gone for his alleged role in the Priority Development Assistance Fund (PDAF) and the Disbursement Acceleration Program (DAP), which had both been declared illegal by the Supreme Court. In addition, Enrile has vowed to file charges against him for alleged criminal negligence in the SAF 44 massacre in Mamasapano.

There have also been speculations of late that Aquino may be thinking of Poe as an alternative candidate (Plan B) if Roxas' rating did not improve as election nears.

For example, some media men and political observers noted that Poe was "going easy" on Aquino during the reopening of the Senate investigation into the Mamasapano massacre. When asked if she thought the President did not do enough to save the SAF troopers from the bloody Mamasapano clash, Poe seemed to offer an excuse for Aquino when she said that since the President was preoccupied most of the time, it should be the responsibility of the Philippine National Police chief to feed him accurate information on what was happening on the ground.

Observers also noted that Poe tried to cut short Enrile's presentation and questioning of witnesses but for the intervention of Sen. Bongbong Marcos, who insisted that Poe allow Enrile to continue. This and Poe's allegedly soft committee report led Enrile to say that "Grace Poe is Aquino's Manchurian candidate," in reference to the movie of the same title, where sinister forces plotted to have their man win the US presidency.

Although very critical of some of Aquino's officials, particularly Transportation Secretary Joseph Emilio Abaya, Poe has been careful not to criticize Aquino, even praising him for his supposed reform agenda.

It must also be noted that despite a pledge by Aquino to join campaign sorties by Roxas and LP vice presidential candidate Rep. Leni Robredo, he has yet to be seen in a single campaign event with Roxas since the start of the year.

Are we seeing a repeat of the betrayal of Roxas in the 2010 vice presidential elections when a group of Aquino leaders, allegedly in conspiracy with the President's sisters, secretly worked for the victory of Binay instead of Roxas, his running mate?

Maybe it is time Roxas distances himself from Aquino and declare his own platform and agenda, and stop saying his victory assures the continuation of the present administration's "daang matuwid." Voters do not want a candidate who will only become a puppet of the present President if he wins.

Ooooo

20

Mamasapano: Let the truth prevail
January 28, 2016

FINALLY, President Aquino did over the weekend what he should have done a year ago. After ignoring – and even doubting – the sacrifice of the 44 members of the Philippine National Police's Special Action Force in the death of international terrorist Zulkifli Bin Hir, alias Marwan, in Mamasapano, Maguindanao on Jan. 25, 2015, the President finally honored the 44 SAF commandos who were mercilessly massacred by Moro Islamic Liberation Front (MILF) rebels after successfully carrying out their mission of either capturing or eliminating Marwan.

Aquino presented posthumous Medal of Valor (Medalya ng Kagitingan) awards to two of the 44 and the PNP Distinguished Conduct Medal (Medalya ng Kabayanihan) to the 42 others who died in that tragic incident.

It was a 180-degree departure from the President's stance regarding the bungled operation that eventually derailed the passage of his Mindanao peace initiative, the Bangsamoro Basic Law, and dashed his hopes of winning the improbable Nobel Peace Prize, not to mention a big drop in his trust and approval ratings.

Prior to Monday's commemoration of the Mamasapano clash, the President was not particularly supportive of the SAF 44 as shown by his actions following the incident. He skipped the arrival honors for the dead troopers in favor of a previously scheduled event at a car manufacturing plant in Paranaque. In his final State-of-the-Nation Address (SONA) in July, Aquino boasted as one of his accomplishments the killing of Marwan but failed to mention SAF's role in the operation. In July, Aquino was reported to have ordered the removal of the mural depicting the heroism of the 44 commandos from the wall of the Philippine National Police Academy. And then in August, Malacanang reportedly ordered the removal of the names of one member of the SAF 44 and a Mamasapano survivor from the roster of recipients of the highest service medals of the PNP.

The moves were seen as an attempt by Malacanang to erase the memory of the bungled Mamasapano operation, although in my opinion, they were futile attempts by a vindictive leader to punish the SAF and its members for causing a serious dent on his leadership, credibility and integrity, not to mention the damage the incident caused on his Mindanao peace initiatives. And then, Senate Minority Leader Juan Ponce Enrile decided it would be to the benefit of the country if the people knew the truth as to what really transpired in Mamasapano on that fateful day and to what extent Aquino was responsible for the death of the SAF 44. We have no doubt that Enrile was out for revenge after he was jailed and humiliated for his alleged complicity in the billion-peso pork barrel scam or that politics could be a motive for reopening the Senate probe on Mamasapano. But still, the people and, more importantly, the families of the fallen heroes need to know the truth. It was not the first time the senators felt the need to revisit Mamasapano. In September, long after the Senate investigative committee headed by now presidential candidate Sen. Grace Poe had submitted its report finding the President "ultimately responsible" for the bungled operation and the massacre of the SAF 44 commandos, several senators, including Poe, said they would reopen the Senate investigation after Aquino hinted of an "alternative truth" on the Mamasapano incident.

In a talk with Inquirer editors in September last year, Aquino said he has been pondering on what he considered an "alternative truth" on the

Mamasapano incident. He said there was an "alternative version of events that happened there, which is undergoing intense scrutiny" and that Malacanang was "looking for witnesses who will prove or disprove certain observations." Aquino was apparently referring to a report on the Mamasapano incident by the MILF that claimed, among other things, that Marwan was killed by one of his aides, and not by the SAF commandos. That Aquino gave credence to MILF's obviously biased report instead of relying on the official report of the PNP's Board of Inquiry rubbed a few more salt to the injury that the relatives of the SAF 44 and the survivors of the debacle have had to endure since the tragic incident. Director Benjamin Magalong, the former chief of the PNP Criminal Investigation and Detection Group (CIDG) who headed the board of inquiry that investigated the botched SAF operation, was incensed by Aquino's giving credence to the MILF claim.

Magalong said that apart from being an attack on the PNP's credibility, the claim that the SAF was not the killer of Marwan was an insult to the 44 police commandos who died in the daylong gun battle with Moro rebels, including fighters from the MILF.

The Board of Inquiry report said President Aquino gave the go-signal to arrest two terrorists and allowed then PNP chief Alan Purisima to participate in the plan despite his suspension. The report said Aquino also bypassed the police's command structure when he directly dealt with former Special Action Force commander Getulio

Napeñas instead of PNP officer-in-charge Leonardo Espina regarding the operation.

Faced with strong criticism, Aquino kept quiet again after that. His advisers probably reminded him that the sooner the people forget about the incident, the better for him.

After Enrile claimed in open plenary session that he had strong evidence to show that Aquino was "directly involved" and allowed 44 Special Action Force (SAF) commandos to be slaughtered, an unidentified police general was quoted by The Standard as saying that Aquino conspired with the military and ordered the Army to stand down so as not to jeopardize the immediate passage of the Bangsamoro Basic Law.

Later, presidential aspirant Davao City Mayor Rodrigo Duterte said he now knows more about the massacre after discussions with military officials who had knowledge of the debacle, revealing that the SAF 44 were "thrown into the lion's lair" without the necessary wherewithal.

Retired Chief Supt. Diosdado Valeroso, meanwhile, claimed over the weekend that he had a digital audio recording of a supposed conversation between a "ranking government official" and a "lawmaker" who appeared to be talking about an alleged attempt to cover up the bloody clash "to avoid its possible effect on the passage of the proposed Bangsamoro Basic Law."

After the Senate agreed to reopen the investigation amid claims by Enrile, Duterte and Valeroso, Malacanang decided to make that incredulous 180-degree turn. Suddenly, the 44

SAF commandos deserved recognition and their families various financial and other benefits. Such hypocrisy!

While obviously happy of the recognition and benefits, the widows and relatives of the fallen SAF 44 did not smile nor thanked Aquino. More than anything else, these people, just like the rest of us, want the truth. The new Senate probe offers a welcome relief from the contentious campaign leading to the May presidential elections and, more importantly, gives us a glimpse of the truth oo what really happened in Mamasapano that fateful day one year ago.

Ooooo

21

Compassion not Aquino's strength
January 21, 2016

PRESIDENT Aquino was just being consistent when he vetoed House Bill No. 5842 that would provide a P2,000 across-the-board increase in the monthly pension of Social Security System (SSS) pensioners. After all, it was not the first time this scion of hacenderos has rejected relief for the millions of poor families in the country.

In 2013, Aquino, who never had to worry about where to get the money to put food on the table, to pay bills, or to buy much-needed medicine much less how to survive in old age, rejected the proposed Magna Carta for the Poor that would give the poor equal access to basic rights and government services. Aquino rejected it on the ground that some of the provisions of the bill were unrealistic, specifically the provision that seeks to provide shelter to the poor that, he said, would need P2.31 trillion to implement.

Aquino also rejected a proposal from Sen. Sonny Angara that would provide income tax cuts for 15 million wage earners.

An income tax cut, according to retired SSS executive vice president and chief actuarian Horacio Templo, would immediately result in a higher net pay for the wage earner. This, he said, would allow the worker to level up his SSS contribution to that of his employer from 3.63 to 7.37 percent of pay and contribute based on his entire salary and beyond the present maximum cap of P16,000. These additional contributions would shore up the Social Security Fund and enable SSS to increase its monthly pensions by P2,000, Templo added.

But Aquino would have none of it. "Will lowering income taxes do good to our countrymen? I am not convinced at the present," Aquino said. "If we lower income tax rates, revenues will be smaller while the deficit will be wider. The widening deficit will be a negative factor when credit rating agencies rate us." Aquino was willing to cut income tax rates if the value-added tax (VAT) would be increased, ignoring the fact that a new round of VAT hikes would trigger higher price increases that would certainly break the backs of the already suffering masses.

And now, despite the public clamor for an increase in the meager monthly pensions being received by some 2 million pensioners, Aquino flatly rejected it with a veto last week. In his veto message, Aquino said if the pension increase were granted, the SSS Investment Reserve Fund (IRF) would have to be tapped and that would bring the IRF to zero balance by 2029, therefore, he said, endangering the stability of the SSS and the pensions of future retirees.

Shrewdly using the divide-and-rule tactic, Aquino sought to pair the 2 million present pensioners against the some 31 million still working and paying monthly contributions by saying that to be able to pay the P2,000 increase, the monthly premiums of those still working would have to be raised or the SSS funds would be so depleted by 2029, they might not get any pension at all.

Aquino and the SSS officials conveniently forgot to mention that in January 2013, the SSS increased the members' monthly premiums by 0.6 percent (from 10.4 percent to 11 percent) of their monthly pay. How come it was so easy for them to increase the contributions of 31 million members and too difficult to grant even a meager pension increase to 2 million pensioners? What are they doing with the money collected from the increased premiums?

And why was it so easy for senior SSS officials to grant themselves millions in bonuses and so easy for Aquino to defend the annual yearend perks? Do they even have a small sense of delicadeza?

The SSS officials have been complaining that there may not be enough funds to ensure the payment of the members' pension in the future unless it increases the members' contribution.

And yet, Salvosa and SSS president Emilio de Quiros said its board members are being paid hefty bonuses every year because the agency meets 90% of its target income every year. If it regularly meets 90% of its annual target income, I see no reason why the SSS funds would not be enough to pay members' pensions "for eternity," as De Quiros likes to describe it, and pay the proposed P2,000 increases.

But no, instead of acceding to the repeated pleas of members to increase their pensions, the SSS board insensitively announced in 2013 that members' contributions would be increased starting in January that year from 10.4 percent of the member's salary to a whopping 11 percent. To those board members, the 0.6-percent difference is nothing but to millions of hard-pressed members, that amount would mean less food on the table.

It is the SSS board and officer's duty to invest the members' money wisely. With billions of pesos in members' contribution coming in annually, there is no reason the pension fund would be depleted if the SSS board and officers make the right decisions on investments and spending.

If they were so good performance-wise to earn the hefty bonuses, how come they don't have enough to pay the proposed increases and how come members have been complaining of very slow processing of death, disability and retirement benefits. Despite its touted computerization, the processing and payment remain "snail-paced," as the Commission on Audit described it.

The COA rejected the SSS justification of excellent performance for granting its board members hefty bonuses. In its 2012 annual report of the state-run firm, the COA noted serious performance issues against the SSS, including the "snail-paced payment of death, disability and retirement benefits."

The SSS should follow the COA admonition that the SSS management should swiftly take legal steps in collecting over P367 million in premiums and penalties from 139 delinquent corporations and employers that have been remiss in their responsibility under the SSS law. In 2011, the COA also expressed dissatisfaction over SSS performance when it assailed its officials for imposing on borrowers interest on loans that exceeded P788.8 million. Imagine an agency that should promote the welfare of its members charging huge interest on salary and emergency loans, among others? That's frying the members with their own lard, so to speak.

The last time the SSS granted an increase in monthly pensions was in 2007, and not a single adjustment to inflation has been made since Aquino's appointees in the SSS board, led by president Emilio de Quiroz Jr. and chairman Johnny Santos, took over in 2010. And on Monday, De Quiroz made it clear there would be no pension increases for the remaining five months of Aquino's term. And he seemed proud of his announcement. What gall!

Not a single pension increase during their six-year watch at SSS, but P10 million worth of bonuses every single year for six years for the Aquino appointees in the board. Talk of the people being their "bosses."

What can P1,200 a month or even P2,400, which are way below the poverty line, in pensions do to help an aging retiree survive, much less live life comfortably? With the continually rising increases in the prices of goods and services, that amount would probably last for a few days, not even counting the amount he has to spend for medicine, which at that age, becomes a daily necessity.

In criticizing the presidential veto, retired Lingayen Archbishop Oscar V. Cruz said, "The President has no mercy, insensitive and unmerciful to the people who have less in life."

Mania Auxiliary Bishop Broderick Pabillo, on the other hand, said in vetoing the SSS pension hike bill, the President showed that his program of inclusive growth is a mere rhetoric.

In his almost six years as president, we have known that Aquino has a few admirable qualities, and compassion for the poor is not among them.

Ooooo

22

Why I Publish/Reprint Books

Tatay Jobo Elizes
Self-Publisher

Writings are timeless and they act as mirrors to history. I publish writings as they remain relevant anytime. I have seen a lot of good writings in the internet, in magazines and newspapers. But most writers have only one or two articles and therefore not enough material to be published as a book. And yet, many of them need to be published or archived. There are also writers who write a lot but never publish them. There are also old books with no more prints available. The solution is to publish/reprint.

I do this for free because of the print-books-on-demand (POD) system, but the printed or hardcopy is not free

The printed book will always be there among your collections or libraries. Not all use the internet. The internet access has its technical problems. I can produce fiction, non-fiction, in color also.

My booklist can be seen at http://tinyurl.com/mj76ccq (copy and paste)

Permission had been granted by the author/authors to print their books under my free self-publishing service. They own copyrights to their works.

Interested reader may request free reading of any of my books, articles or essays via online reading or ebook. Just select and email me. Thank you.

ooooo